DATE DUE

NOV 2 4 1980			
DEC 1 1980			
OCT 1 2 1981			
NOV 9 1981			
NOV 3 0 1981			
NOV 3 0 1981			
NOV 2 9 1982			
GAYLORD 234			PRINTED IN U. S. A.

Death of a Nation

Discovery Books

Death of a Nation

16357

Ray C. Stedman

Word Books, Publisher

Waco, Texas

DEATH OF A NATION

Discovery Books are published by Word Books,
Publisher in cooperation with Discovery Foundation,
Palo Alto, California.
ISBN 0–87680–458–X
Library of Congress catalog card number: 75–36190

Printed in the United States of America

OTHER BOOKS IN THE DISCOVERY SERIES:

Authentic Christianity
Jesus Teaches on Prayer
Spiritual Warfare
Understanding Man
Love Story . . . the Real Thing
Dying to Live
Behind History
Family Life
A Nation Under God?

Contents

Introduction

The tragedy of Judah, as it unfolds in the pages of the Book of Jeremiah, is the tragedy of nations today. This Book of Jeremiah, though written thousands of years ago, is still as relevant, up-to-date and pertinent to our day as it was when first written. The tragedy is that when people forsake God they lose the sense of their own worth. Without exception, when someone turns from God he also loses himself. When the people of Judah turned from the living fountain of God they became like animals, Jeremiah said. They began to act brutishly, and thus to hate themselves. This is always the consequence of a heart which rejects or turns from the living God. When you lose God, you no longer can love yourself. And if you cannot love yourself, you cannot love your neighbor. That reflects the wisdom of the great commandment Jesus gave us: "Love your neighbor as yourself." If you have no sense of who you are as a person, then you will not look at anyone else as a person, either. So the tragedy of this nation was that it had begun to lose its sense of God, and thus had begun to lose its sense of self.

The Book of Jeremiah is set in a time of crisis and moral decline of the nation. It reveals what is behind the death of a nation. In many ways, we are facing the parallel of Judah's experience in our day. In 1976 our nation celebrates its two-hundredth birthday. Many feel that as we celebrate our Bicentennial we also may be witnesses to the beginning of the end of the United States of America. I hope it is not true. But the forces which are destroying our nation are the same forces which destroyed the nation to which Jeremiah witnessed. We can learn a great deal about what is going on in our nation by studying this great prophecy of Jeremiah. We can learn here how to behave in a time of national and personal crisis. What should a believer do when things are falling apart around him in his home, his community, his nation, and the world in which he lives? The answers are here. And from this prophecy we will also learn what is the word of hope in an hour of despair and darkness, and how God plants the seeds of new life in the midst of death and destruction.

1

Called for a Crisis

In this series of studies on the Book of Jeremiah, I do not intend to examine every verse, but rather to capture the thought and message of this great prophecy and bring it before your minds and hearts. There is much to learn from Jeremiah. I have come to love this book greatly and I think you will, too.

Perhaps you are not familiar with the book. Jeremiah is not the greatest of the prophets. Isaiah, I think, would be awarded that distinction. Nor is Jeremiah the most difficult of the prophets to understand. Ezekiel would probably qualify there. But of all the prophets, surely Jeremiah is the most heroic. This young man began his ministry in the days of Josiah the king of Judah, and for forty-two years he preached in Judah, trying to awaken the nation to what was about to happen to it. He tried to get them to turn around, to save them from the judgment of God. But in all those forty-two years he never once saw any sign of encouragement. His preaching in no way deterred the headlong rush of this nation toward its own destruction. Never did he see any sign that what he was saying had any impact at all upon these people.

And yet, he was faithful to his task. Through much personal sorrow, struggle, heartache, difficulty and danger, he performed what God had sent him to do. And in so doing, he left a tremendous record of the greatness of God, of his power over nations and his control of history, and of the hope which arises out of darkness.

In the opening chapter we have a full-length portrait of the prophet, and of the times in which he lived. The first three verses set the prophecy in its historical background:

> The words of Jeremiah, the son of Hilkiah, of the priests who were in Anathoth in the land of Benjamin, to whom the word of the Lord came in the days of Josiah the son of Amon, king of Judah, in the thirteenth year of his reign. It came also in the days of Jehoiakim the son of Josiah, king of Judah, and until the end of the eleventh year of Zedekiah, the son of Josiah, king of Judah, until the captivity of Jerusalem in the fifth month (Jer. 1:1–3).

That is a bare-bones description of the circumstances and the times in which Jeremiah ministered. It does not give us much of the flavor of those days, but these were troubled times in the nation. Israel, the Northern Kingdom, had already been carried into captivity by Assyria a hundred years earlier. Now Judah, the Southern Kingdom, was rushing blindly along a course which was certain to lead it to the same judgment. It was during the reign of Josiah, the last good and godly king of Judah, that Jeremiah began his ministry.

The prophecy of Jeremiah is a collection of his messages, interspersed with historical narrative which provides background. It does not proceed chronologically, but jumps from here to there in place and back and forth in time. The moral progress through the book, however, is very orderly, and it is that which we will follow. It began in the days of Josiah, and ended in the days of his son, Zedekiah, the last king of Judah, with the exile of Judah under the Babylonians.

Jeremiah is introduced to us as the son of a priest. He was what we might call a "P.K.," a preacher's kid, growing up in the town of Anathoth where only priests lived. His father's name was Hilkiah, which is a very common name, but some scholars think that Jeremiah's father may have been the same Hilkiah who was high priest in the days of Josiah.

The Book of 2 Kings tells us that this Hilkiah was rummaging around in the rooms of the temple one day, looking over some old records and money boxes which had been stored there for years, and down underneath a lot of dusty ledgers he found a scroll. He brought it out, cleaned it off, and began to read it. To his amazement he discovered that it was a copy of the Law of Moses! The nation had fallen so far that the Law had actually been lost and forgotten. Hilkiah was stunned by what he read. He sent the scroll to Josiah the king, who was also astonished, and frightened that the wrath of God would be poured out on them because they had not kept the Law. He made a covenant before the Lord to keep his commandments, and took away all the idol abominations, beginning what was to be the last national reform this nation experienced before its exile.

Witness to Disaster

Whether or not this Hilkiah was Jeremiah's father, Jeremiah began his ministry under Josiah the king, in the days when Josiah was trying desperately to set the kingdom right. But although Josiah moved with great authority and power to tear down the idols and restore the worship of Jehovah, the reform was merely transitory. As soon as the king died, everything deteriorated once more. After Josiah died, Jehoahaz, Josiah's son, after ruling for three months, was captured by Egypt and carried away into exile. Jeremiah watched Assyria's might, in the north, being crushed by the power of Babylon. Then Egypt was humbled by Babylon at the Battle of Carchemish in 605 B.C., one of the strategic battles of all time. Jeremiah saw the total domination of the world by Babylon, under King Nebuchadnezzar. At last he saw the invasion of his own beloved land of Judah by the Babylonian armies, the surrounding of Jerusalem, the siege of the city, and its downfall. He saw the people of Judah carried away into Babylonian captivity, and he was left in a desolated land, a land utterly ravaged by war. Then, betrayed by politicians, he was taken as a captive to Egypt where he died unknown, unhonored, and unsung. Tradition tells us he was stoned to death by the very Jews whom he trusted as brothers.

Here was a man, then, who knew nothing of the outward encouragement of success. He was never to see his prophecies of healing and health for the land fulfilled. And yet, despite all this, he was absolutely faithful to the call of God. The heroism and courage of this man have become a source of great encouragement to my own heart.

In the next few verses is found the call of Jeremiah by God. It is a remarkable account of how God prepared and sent this young man into a ministry. God does the calling, does the preparing, and provides the power. It is all of God. Notice the *preparation* of God:

Now the word of the Lord came to me saying,
"Before I formed you in the womb I knew you,
and before you were born I consecrated you;
I appointed you a prophet to the nations" (Jer. 1:4–5).

Isn't it remarkable that when God began to talk to this young man, the first thing he did was to sit down and share with him the Four Spiritual Laws?—at least the first one: "God loves you and has a wonderful plan for your life." Isn't that what he is saying? "Before I formed you in the womb I knew you, and before you were born I consecrated you; I appointed you a prophet to the nations." This is the preparation of God, and it had begun long before Jeremiah was even conceived. In other words, God said, "I started getting you ready, and the world ready for you, long before you were born. I worked through your father and your mother, your grandfathers and grandmothers, your great-grandfathers and great-grandmothers. For generations I have been preparing you." What a wonderful revelation to this young man!

Before You Were Born

When men face a crisis, they always start looking for a program, some method with which to attack the crisis. But when God sets out to solve a crisis, he almost always starts with a baby. The babies God sends into the world, who look so innocent and so helpless—and so useless at their birth—have enormous potential. There is nothing very impressive in appearance about a baby, but that is God's way of changing the world. Hidden in the heart of a baby are the most amazing possibilities. That is what God said to Jeremiah: "I've been working before you were born to prepare you to be a prophet, working through your father and your mother, and those who were before them."

History tells us that the mother of Sir Walter Scott loved poetry and art, so it's not surprising that her son became a poet. The mother of Lord Byron was hot-tempered, proud, and violent. The mother of Napoleon Bonaparte was ambitious for herself and her children. The mother of John and Charles Wesley was a godly and devout woman, with great executive ability—and, having nineteen children, she needed it! God prepares for a child long before that child is born.

God prepares for *every* child in this way; the kind of preparation spoken of in this passage doesn't apply only to Jeremiah the prophet. I often hear people say of some noted person, "When God made him, he broke the mold." That is true. When God made Abraham Lincoln he broke the mold. There has never been another like him. But what we often fail to see is that this is true of every single one of us; there is nothing unusual about it. God never made another one like you, and he never will. God never made anyone else who can fill the place you can fill and do the things you can do. This is the wonder of the way God forms human life—that of the billions who have lived on this earth there are no duplicates. Each one is unique, prepared of God for the time in which he is to live. To strengthen Jeremiah, God said to him, "I have prepared you for this very hour," just as he has prepared you and me for this time, for this world, for this hour of human history.

Each of us, therefore, is both the goal toward which God has been working and, at the same time, the preparation of others yet to come, for we have a part in their work as well. Not long ago, I heard the story of the death of a young pastor. When he was dying of cancer, his father and uncle, both of whom are pastors, came to see him. After visiting with them both a short while, the young man asked his uncle, "Would you mind if I talk to my dad alone?" When the father came out, he and his brother went to get some coffee, and the father said, "I want to tell you what David did while we were alone. He called me over to his bed and said, 'Can I put my arms around you?' I stooped over as best I could and let him put his arms around me. 'And now, dad, would you put your arms around me?' I could hardly keep control of my emotions, but I put my arms around him. Then, with his arms around me, he said, 'Dad, I just want you to know that the greatest gift God ever gave me, outside of salvation itself, was the gift of a father and mother who love God and taught me to love him, too.' "

That is what God is saying to Jeremiah. "What a gift you have! How I have prepared you for this moment, through the generations which lie behind you, that you might live and speak and act in this time in history."

Shrinking Prophet

But beyond the preparation of God, there is also the *provision* of God:

> Then I said, "Ah, Lord God! Behold, I do not know how to speak, for I am only a youth." But the Lord said to me,
> "Do not say, 'I am only a youth' ";
> for to all to whom I send you you shall go,
> and whatever I command you you shall speak.
> Be not afraid of them,
> for I am with you to deliver you,
>   says the Lord" (Jer. 1:6–8).

Jeremiah's response is to shrink from the call of God. Many a young man had done that before him—Moses, Gideon, Isaiah, and other mighty men of God. When God first laid hold of them and set them to a task, they shrank from it. Jeremiah pleads youth and inexperience, and says he has no ability to speak, just as Moses did. So if you ever feel fearful and inadequate when God calls you to a task, just remember that you are in the prophetic succession! God's men often start out that way.

As far as we can tell, Jeremiah was about thirty years old when God called him. That is when young men began their ministry in Judah. By the standards of modern youth, that would be considered over the hill, beyond the time a man is capable of starting anything. But that is when God often starts. Jesus was thirty years old when he began his ministry. Yet Jeremiah is acutely aware of his inadequacy and his inexperience, which, I think, indicates the sensitivity of this young man. Throughout the whole prophecy you find him very responsive and sensitive to what is happening to him. He is called to stand before kings, to thunder denunciations and judgments, to feel the sharp lash of their recrimination against him, to endure their anger and their power, and to suffer with his people as he sees them rushing headlong to their own self-destruction. We know he feels this keenly and sharply for the Book of Lamentations is made up of the cries of his heart as he senses all that is happening to him.

But God answers Jeremiah in the same way he has answered every other young man who felt this way: "Go, for I am with you. Don't worry about your voice, your looks, your personality, your ability—*I* will be with you. I will be your voice. I'll speak through you, give you the words. I'll give you the power to stand. I'll give you the courage. I'll be your wisdom. I'll be whatever you need. Whatever demand is made upon you, I'll be there to meet it."

Do you recognize that this, essentially, is the New Covenant that Jesus makes with all of us? This is what he promises each one of us—that he will be with us in this same way. The promise which encouraged Jeremiah is the same promise which is handed to us in the gospel. Whatever we are, whatever demand is made upon us, God says, "Do not be afraid. Do not shrink back. Do not say, 'I can't do that.' Remember that I will be with you, and I will make you able to do it."

And so, the third division of this call is the promise of the *power* of God:

> Then the Lord put forth his hand and touched my
> mouth; and the Lord said to me,
> "Behold, I have put my words in your mouth.
> See, I have set you this day over nations and
> over kingdoms,
> to pluck up and to break down,
> to destroy and to overthrow,
> to build and to plant" (Jer. 1:9–10).

As with Isaiah, God touched Jeremiah's mouth. Isaiah started his ministry when God touched his mouth with the coals from the altar and gave him power in speaking. Jeremiah's words, then, become the key to his power, the living, burning, shattering, building, mighty power of the word of God. In this power, Jeremiah was set over nations and kingdoms. This was not mere poetry. The messages of this book were actually addressed to all the great nations of the world of that day—to Egypt, to Assyria, even to Babylon in its towering might and strength. Jeremiah was given a word for all these nations. I like to think of this scene, because I think it is repeated in every generation. Here are the nations of the world, with their obvious display of power and pomp and circumstance, with statesmen and leaders who are well-known household names, marching up and down, threatening one another, rattling their sabers, acting so proud and self-assertive. But God picks out an obscure young man, a youth thirty years of age whom no one has ever heard of, from a tiny little town in a small, obscure country, and says to him, "I have set you over all the nations and kingdoms of the earth. Your word, because it is my word, will have more power than all the power of the nations."

That is a remarkable description of our heritage as believers in Jesus Christ. James says that the prayer of a righteous man releases great power. And when you and I pray about the affairs of life, we can affect the fate of nations, as the word of Jeremiah altered the destiny of the nations of his day, even though we are obscure and no one knows who we are. This has happened before in the course of history.

Destruction with Purpose

So Jeremiah was set in the midst of death and destruction, but God said he would plant a hope and a healing. His word was to "pluck up and to break down, to destroy and to overthrow"—and that is always the work of God. In a nation there are many things which have to be torn down—things men trust in—just as in an individual's heart and life there are things which need to be destroyed. I talked with a young man not long ago who said to me, "I don't understand what's wrong with my marriage. I'm doing everything I know to do, but our relationship isn't right. I can't put my finger on what is wrong." I said to him, "I'm sure there is something wrong, and God will show it to you. There are things you're doing in your marriage which you're not aware of, things you need to see. But right now you are blinded to them. You think things are right, and yet they're not, and it puzzles you. All this indicates is that there are still things God needs to tear down—points of pride, or times of discourtesy, perhaps, that you don't recognize; habits and reactions of worry and anxiety and anger and frustration that you've fallen into or given way to, and you don't even know about them." We all have areas like these in our lives. And the work of God is to open our eyes to these things, to destroy them and root them out . . . and then, always, to build and to plant. God never destroys for the purpose of destroying; he destroys in order to build up again. This was God's word to Jeremiah.

The closing section of this chapter depicts the ministry of this young man in the land. It falls into three major divisions, beginning with verse 11. First there are certain symbols of what would be accomplished through Jeremiah's ministry:

> And the word of the Lord came to me, saying, "Jeremiah, what do you see?" And I said, "I see a rod of almond [i.e., a branch of the almond tree]." Then the Lord said to me, "You have seen well, for I am watching over my word to perform it."

There is a little play on words here, in the Hebrew. The Jews called the almond tree "the watcher" (*shaqed*) because it was the first tree to blossom in the spring. They saw it as watching for the return of the sun and the warming of the earth, and therefore the first to herald the coming of springtime. And God said to Jeremiah, "You have seen well, for that is what I am doing; I am watching (*shaqed*) over my word to perform it." This is a picture of health and healing. Throughout this prophecy there are wonderful passages which deal with the way God was planning to heal this land. For example, Jeremiah was sent to buy a piece of property while the city was being taken by the enemy. In the midst of all this destruction he was to buy this property, get the title deed, and have it sealed and witnessed, as a testimony to the fact that God intended to restore the land, and that property would still be of value. This is what God does also in our lives.

There is another symbol: the boiling pot.

> The word of the Lord came to me a second time, saying, "What do you see?" And I said, "I see a boiling pot, facing away from the north." Then the Lord said to me, "Out of the north evil shall break forth upon all the inhabitants of the land. For, lo, I am calling all the tribes of the kingdoms of the north, says the Lord; and they shall come and every one shall set his throne at the entrance of the gates of Jerusalem, against all its walls round about, and against all the cities of Judah" (Jer. 1:13–15).

The prophet saw a pot boiling, with smoke and steam rising up, streaming in the north wind toward the south. God said, "Jeremiah, that is a picture of what I'm going to do. I'm going to bring a boiling pot—a confederation of nations down from the north against this city of Jerusalem [as he is going to do once more in our day, perhaps very soon], and the city will be taken, its people driven into exile, and my judgment will fall upon this land." This was the picture of judgment. And it was to come from the north. Although Egypt was the greatest power on earth at this time, Egypt is ignored here, and God seizes upon Babylon as the source from which judgment would come.

Signs of Decay

Then, second, he announces the cause of that judgment, verse 16: "And I will utter my judgments against them, for all their wickedness in forsaking me; they have burned incense to other gods, and worshiped the works of their own hands." The reason a nation dies is that it forsakes its God, as evidenced by two things: First, the nation burns incense before other gods; that is, it exalts ideas and philosophies which represent the various controlling passions and imaginations of men. Second, its people worship the works of their own hands; they exalt man, pointing to man as the solution to his own problems—in other words, the rise of humanism. These are the signs of decay in a nation. This is what was happening in Israel. In the very first prophecy of Jeremiah to Judah, chapter 2, verse 13, he says,

> ". . . for my people have committed two evils;
>   they have forsaken me,
> the fountain of living waters,
>   and hewed out cisterns for themselves,
> broken cisterns,
>   that can hold no water."

Here is a valley with a stream running through it, a beautiful mountain stream with clear, cool, clean water. The people have been drinking from that water, but then they forsake it. And up on the barren, rocky hillsides, they hew out cisterns to catch the water as it runs off down the mountainside with its dirt and its leaves and its collection of bugs and dead mice. The cisterns leak. They do not hold the water. So, at great expense, the people are constantly building cisterns which break in the drought and let the water run out so that they are left with nothing to drink, while the stream of living water runs fresh in the valley below.

What a picture that is! A lot of people do that, do they not? They turn from God who is able to bring the freshness and vitality of joy and peace and love into a life, and start seeking satisfaction in all kinds of dead human philosophy, in failing friendships, in momentary pleasures. These are the broken cisterns that can hold no water. This is when a nation, a home, an individual, begins to die.

But in the final section of this first chapter, God gives Jeremiah this promise:

> "But you, gird up your loins; arise, and say to them everything I command you. Do not be dismayed by them, lest I dismay you before them. And I, behold, I make you this day a fortified city, an iron pillar, and bronze walls, against the whole land, against the kings of Judah, its princes, its priests, and the people of the land. They will fight against you; but they shall not prevail against you, for I am with you, says the Lord, to deliver you" (Jer. 1:17–19).

When I was a boy in high school, sixteen years old, I was arrested because it was alleged (wrongly, it was proved) that I had been hunting out of season. I still remember how fearsome it was to receive that warrant for my arrest, to open it up and read these words: "The People of the State of Montana versus Ray C. Stedman." I thought, "What unfair odds! The whole population of the state of Montana against me!" That is what this prophet Jeremiah had to face. All the people of the land, and its kings and priests, would be against him. But God said, "Don't you worry, you shall stand. I'll make you a stone, an iron, and a bronze against them. Nothing will shake you." And the amazing thing is that though this young man was thrown into prison, put in a dungeon where he was mired in the mud, put on a bread-and-water diet, though he was ostracized and isolated, set aside, rejected and insulted, and finally exiled into Egypt, never once when God asked him to speak did he ever fail to say exactly what God told him to say. What remarkable courage this young man exhibited!

Through all of it Jeremiah learned four things: He learned the sovereignty of God, his control over the nations of earth. He learned the ruthlessness of God, whose judgments would be unmerciful against his people who persisted in turning away from him. He learned the faithfulness of God always to fulfill his word, no matter what was said. And finally he learned the tenderness of God, to suffer with the heart of God. He lost hope for a while and cried out, "O that I had never been born!" He felt the awful hurt of his people, and wept over them. But through it all he realized that what he was feeling was the suffering of the heart of God over people who turn him aside, and the tenderness of God that draws them back at last, despite all their wandering. That is the prophecy of Jeremiah. I hope you will enjoy it as we go through it together, and learn much for the hour of our own national peril.

2

The Way Back

The first message of Jeremiah to the nation of Judah covers several chapters, but I want to pick out certain passages which highlight for us what God has to say to someone who has begun to drift away from him. Have you ever had that problem? I have. I find there are times in my life when, without even realizing it, I have begun to lose some of the fervor, joy, and peace which mark the presence of God flowing through my life.

The tragic thing about that condition, as exemplified in the nation of Judah, is that when it happens nobody knows what is wrong. Judah really blamed God for all the problems they were having, just as most of us do. They said it was God's fault; he did not deliver them when he ought to, and did not keep them from their enemies as he promised. They were charging him with gross misconduct and with inability to keep his promises.

So God has something to say to this nation, and what he says gathers around four words that Jeremiah uses: remember, realize, return, and beware. I hope you will take these four words as an instruction to your own heart about how to get back to God. Use them when you sense somehow that you have begun to drift, or that you have lost some of the flavor and the joy of your Christian experience. The first word is found in chapter 2:

> The word of the Lord came to me, saying, "Go and proclaim in the hearing of Jerusalem, Thus says the Lord,
> I remember the devotion of your youth,
>   your love as a bride,
> how you followed me in the wilderness,
>   in a land not sown.
> Israel was holy to the Lord,
>   the first fruits of his harvest.
> All who ate of it became guilty;
>   evil came upon them,
>   says the Lord" (Jer. 2:1–3).

The first word is *remember*. That is a look back, a call to remember what life was like when you first began a love relationship. God says, "I remember the devotion of your youth, your love as a bride, how you followed me." In marital counseling I have often dealt with couples who have been married twenty-five or thirty years, but who are having difficulties. They are tense, angry, upset, and sometimes they will not even speak to one another. One man was so angry with his wife that he got up, spit in her face, and walked out the door! How do you begin the healing process with couples in such a state?

Long ago I learned the best way is simply to say, "You know, before we start, I need to get acquainted with you a bit. Tell me something about yourselves. How did you meet, and where?" You can feel the atmosphere soften, and their hearts begin to expand a bit, as they think back to the days when they were not angry or upset, and as they remember what it meant to be in love. Half the battle is won when you can get couples thinking back to what it was like when they first knew each other.

Do you remember those days in your relationship with the Lord—the wonder of love, and the joy of it? What the prophet is bringing out here is that at such a time, the loved one is the chief priority in life. No other relationship is more important than yours with him, or hers with you. He is preeminent in your affection. Therefore, the first thing God says to a heart which has begun to drift is, "Remember, remember what is was like when you were secure in my affections, separate unto me?"

A young man who was with me on a trip recently told me that he had listened to someone speak on the letters to the seven churches in Revelation 2:4. When the speaker got to what the Lord Jesus said to the angel of the church in Ephesus—"I have this against you, that you have left your first love"—this young man said something gripped his heart. It was as though scales dropped from his eyes. And he suddenly realized that he had come to love Bible study *about* Jesus more than he loved *Jesus himself*. He saw that he had to return to that "first love," and that Bible study, engaging and exciting as it is, is not what holds the heart. It is Jesus himself. And that is what God says—"Remember, Judah, those days in the wilderness when you walked as a bride with her husband, how you were safe, and satisfied, and exclusively mine."

Know and See

The second word which God uses to try to arrest this people is found in chapter 2, verse 19:

> "Your wickedness will chasten you,
> and your apostasy will reprove you.

> Know and see that it is evil and bitter
>   for you to forsake the Lord your God;
>   the fear of me is not in you,
>   says the Lord God of hosts."

"Know and see." That is a word for the present, is it not? "Look around," God says. "*Realize* where you are and what has happened to you. What are you like, right now? Remember the past, and realize the present. What has happened to you in your life?" This is his way of arresting Judah's attention, of helping them to see how needy they were and how much they needed him. So he says, "Know and see that it is evil and bitter for you to forsake the Lord your God." Several passages are gathered around this word, on which I won't expound in detail, but I do want to point out two vivid illustrations which God holds up to us. God, the master illustrator, uses wonderful visual aids to help us understand truth, and he holds up before Israel two pictures which will help them to see themselves, and will help us to see ourselves as well. The first, which I have mentioned already, is in chapter 2, verse 13:

> ". . . for my people have committed two evils;
>   they have forsaken me,
>   the fountain of living waters,
>   and hewed out cisterns for themselves,
>   broken cisterns,
>   that can hold no water."

God says that is what Judah has been doing, and he details it for them in verse 4:

> Hear the word of the Lord, O house of Jacob,
> and all the families of the house of Israel. Thus
> says the Lord:

"What wrong did your fathers find in me
    that they went far from me,
and went after worthlessness, and became
    worthless?" (Jer. 2:4–5).

That is the folly of somebody who forsakes the Lord. Remember how many times in the Scriptures believers are depicted as a river of living water, refreshing, rushing, bringing cleansing and healing and fruit. Jesus spoke of the rivers of healing water that flow from our life when the Spirit of God is ruling. And you know those times, don't you? You have already experienced that inner sense of gladness, of joy, that God is present. Why would anyone forsake that, and try to be satisfied with a lot of cheap things? It would be like forsaking the sunshine and huddling in a cave somewhere, trying to be satisfied with the light of a candle. Or worse, perhaps, it would be like giving up eating and trying to satisfy yourself by drooling over all the food ads in the magazines. That is what God says it is like when you turn from the living God, who alone can satisfy the heart.

Spiritual Harlotry

The other picture I want to mention is even more graphic:

"For long ago you broke your yoke
    and burst your bonds;
    and you said, 'I will not serve.'
Yea, upon every high hill
    and under every green tree
    you bowed down as a harlot.
Yet I planted you a choice vine,
    wholly of pure seed.

> How then have you turned degenerate . . . ?"
>   (Jer. 2:20–21).

When you forsake the living God, it is not very long before deterioration and degeneracy set in, and you become available to any and every drive and force around you. God calls that harlotry—spiritual harlotry. He asks a searching question in verses 23 and 24:

> "How can you say, 'I am not defiled,
>   I have not gone after the Baals'?
> Look at your way in the valley;
>   know what you have done—
> a restive young camel interlacing her tracks,
>   a wild ass used to the wilderness,
> in her heat sniffing the wind!
>   Who can restrain her lust?
> None who seek her need weary themselves;
>   in her month they will find her" (Jer. 2:23–24).

Do you see the picture? If you have ever worked among horses you know what he is talking about. Here is a mare in heat, lusting. A little later on in chapter 5 he speaks of lusty stallions who keep neighing after their neighbors' wives. God uses these vivid figures to awaken people to where they are. There is a wonderful frankness about the Scriptures which sometimes rebukes the Victorian prudishness to which we have fallen heir. God intended us to learn from the animal kingdom. He gave animals a different kind of sexuality than he gave us, in order that we might learn from them. In observing them, we have a vivid picture of how we look when we start lusting after everything that comes along, making ourselves available for any kick, any thrill, any drive, other than God himself.

This picture must have meant a great deal to the people

of Judah. They understood how an animal looks in heat, how eager it is to be satisfied. I remember a scene from my high school days, when I was working on a ranch in Montana. One day a group of people came out from town to go horseback riding. Among them were some school-teachers, and one was my English teacher, who was something of an old maid. I remember that she was given a stallion to ride, and when we were saddling up, the stallion got tremendously excited about a nearby mare. To this day I can vividly recall the bright crimson of her face as she sat on that horse, while everybody else tried to pretend nothing was happening! But God uses this figure to say to us, "That is what you're like. That is you, lusting after everything that comes by, living for kicks, wanting to be satisfied by everything from continuous, nonstop television, or endless golf, to the fleshpots of the city, to heroin, to hate and violence." That is what happens when the heart begins to drift from God into degeneracy.

The First Step Back

The third word for us, in tracing the way back to God, is repeated several times in Jeremiah's prophecy. For example:

> And the Lord said to me, "Faithless Israel has shown herself less guilty than false Judah. Go, and proclaim these words toward the north, and say,
> 'Return, faithless Israel,
> says the Lord.
> I will not look on you in anger,
> for I am merciful,
> says the Lord;
> I will not be angry for ever'" (Jer. 3:11–12).

The word is *return*. He says it again in verse 22: "Return, O faithless sons, I will heal your faithlessness." And in chapter 4: "If you return, O Israel, says the Lord, to me you should return" (vs. 1). If you are going down a road, and find that you are on the wrong road, the only logical thing to do is to turn around and go back to where you lost your way. That is what we find so hard to do, because of the first step we must take, which is clearly described in chapter 3, verse 13:

"Only acknowledge your guilt,
     that you rebelled against the Lord your God
and scattered your favors among strangers under every green
     tree,
     and that you have not obeyed my voice,
                                         says the Lord."

That is the tough part, is it not? "Only acknowledge your guilt." God sees the heart, and we cannot fool him. We can justify ourselves, and excuse ourselves to those around us, but we cannot fool the living God who is waiting to refresh us and heal us, waiting until we have acknowledged our guilt. I am concerned when Christians sometimes treat the beautiful promises of forgiveness in the New Testament as though they were automatic. They seem to have the idea that God is so ready to forgive that the minute you do something wrong he instantly forgives you, and it does not matter whether you acknowledge your guilt or not. But that is not biblical. I do not think it is right to use 1 John 1:9—"If we confess our sins, he is faithful and just, and will forgive our sins and cleanse us from all unrighteousness"—as if forgiveness simply happens automatically whenever you do anything wrong. God does not want us to confess and acknowledge our

guilt for *his* sake; it is for *our* sake that we are to do it, so
that we might see what was wrong and learn from it. So
God says that the way to return is to acknowledge our
guilt.

Stuart Briscoe told me once of an incident in his church.
A young boy had come to Christ through some of the
people in the church who had reached out to him while
he was on drugs. They were so loving and gracious to him
as they led him to Christ that he was eager to come to
church. He did come, and later asked to be a member of
the church. On the morning he was to be accepted into
membership, he asked if he could say a few words to the
congregation. Stuart Briscoe agreed, so the young man
stood up and said, "I just want to tell you something about
myself. I was on drugs; I was all fouled up; I was a mess.
I hated myself. Then some people from this church met
me, and they loved me as I've never been loved before.
They told me about Jesus, and I found Jesus. I was so
eager to come to this church, because these people were
from here. I came here because I wanted to see a church
that could put out people like that.

"But I was so disappointed! You didn't like my long
hair, and I could feel it in your glances. I could sense your
hostility when you pointedly ignored me. I could see that
some of you were downright angry because I was present
among you. It made me very resentful. I got bitter and
angry at you because you were like that. I just want to tell
you that God has dealt with my heart, and I realize that
it is wrong for me to be bitter and angry at you. Now,
your hostility toward me—that is your own problem before God. You will have to settle that. But I just want to
say that I was wrong in being angry with you. God has
forgiven me, and I ask you to forgive me, and to receive

me into membership here." That is a good example of what God is after, the acknowledgment of guilt.

God goes on to say, in verse 15, " 'And I will give you shepherds after my own heart, who will feed you with knowledge and understanding.' " Do you see how he is reaching after these people? "Return," he says. "Come back. It is not too late. I will restore you, I will feed you, I will open your eyes. You will not have to walk in ignorance and darkness again. I will heal your faithlessness."

What About the End?

But there is one more word here, and because Jeremiah found it necessary to add it, so must we. The word is *beware*. In chapter 5, verse 29, God says,

> "Shall I not punish them for these things?
>
> says the Lord,
>
> and shall I not avenge myself
> on a nation such as this?"
> An appalling and horrible thing
> has happened in the land:
> the prophets prophesy falsely,
> and the priests rule at their direction;
> my people love to have it so,
> [and then comes this word of warning—]
> but what will you do when the end comes?
> (Jer. 5:29–31).

Jesus said that life is like building a house. You can build it two ways: you can build on the rock, as do those who hear his words, and love and obey him; or you can build it on the sand, that is, based on any system of thought or philosophy other than Jesus. You can erect a beautiful house on either place, one that looks attractive to others.

But a testing time is coming. And when the winds come and the waves beat against the house, the house which is built on the rock will stand, while the house which is built on the sand will fall, no matter how useful or apparently comfortable it has been.

The question God is asking you and me now is this: What about the end? Perhaps you have been going to church for years, but you have never really come to Christ. Or perhaps you have come to Christ, but you have drifted away. God says that he has made a way back, but there is only one way: acknowledge your guilt. God will heal your faithlessness. But if you do not, there is nothing else but to go on to worse conditions, until there comes an end. I do not know what the end would be for you. I do not know where you are. I do know this: my heart says to me, "I want to come back to the God who loves me, the God who can heal me, the God who opens the fountains of living water to refresh my heart and spirit, and I want to walk with him."

3

Love's Last Resort

Jeremiah's second message in his ministry to Judah was delivered about five years after the first, in the eighteenth year of king Josiah. The message has a different content than the first, as we will see in a moment, but the really startling thing about this passage is the effect it has upon the prophet himself.

I have discovered that the most baffling times in my experience as a Christian have been when God begins to act completely contrary to the way I expect. When God seems difficult to handle, then things really toughen up in the Christian experience! There are times when God apparently ignores his promises, even changes his character, and does not act the way I assume he should.

We all like to put God in a box, to program him. And we do it quite honestly. We have studied the Scriptures—his own revelation. We have picked out certain promises he has given. We say that he is bound to act by these, and so we expect him to act on those terms. But to our utter dismay and chagrin he ignores our program and acts entirely differently.

Stop Praying

Of course the problem is that we have picked just a part of what he has to say. None of us is big enough to see God in balance. And this was Jeremiah's problem in this message, for God told this young man to do two astonishing things. The first is given to us in verse 16 of chapter 7. God says to the prophet, "As for you, do not pray for this people, or lift up cry or prayer for them, and do not intercede with me, for I do not hear you." Imagine that! God commanded the prophet to cease praying for the people of Judah, and not to ask God for their deliverance any longer. He was not to cry out to God for them, to fast, pray, nor in any other way to intercede on behalf of these people. God says, "Don't pray." Most of us think of prayer as something to do when everything else fails. And surely the last thing God would ever command is that we stop praying!

If you are given to picking out favorite texts from Scripture, as so many are, and saying, "*This* is the way God is going to act," you are going to have trouble with verses like this. There is a passage in 1 Samuel in which Samuel is sent by God to tell the nation Israel that they have turned from him and rejected him as king. Israel has demanded a king like all the other nations around, and Samuel says that God will accede to their request and give them a king, but that they will not like it. Then Samuel says these words: "Moreover as for me, far be it from me that I should sin against the Lord by ceasing to pray for you . . ." (1 Sam. 12:23). Many times we quote that as the teaching of the Bible about prayer. But then what do you do with a verse like this, where God says to Jeremiah, "As for you, do not pray for this people, or lift up cry or prayer for them, and do not intercede with me, for I do not hear you"?

As if that were not bad enough, in verse 27 God says to the prophet, "So you shall speak all these words to them, but they will not listen to you. You shall call to them, but they will not answer you."

In other words, "Stop praying, Jeremiah, but keep on preaching." Now, that is hard to do! Perhaps you don't think of yourselves as preachers, but anyone who speaks the Word of God to another person is, in a sense, preaching to them. What God is saying to Jeremiah is, "Don't pray, but I want you to keep preaching. And I tell you this: they will not listen to you at all. They won't pay any attention to you. They are just going to go right on their way. But I want you still to stand up and say what you have to say to them." That is one of the roughest assignments ever given to anybody by God. I find there are times when people will not listen to my preaching, and it is a great comfort to me to go home and pray for them when that happens! But Jeremiah could not even do that. There are times when if God said to me, "Stop praying," I would utterly fall apart. Prayer has been a refuge and a strength to me.

I do not think we understand what this is all about unless we look at the historical setting, so let's go back to the beginning of chapter 7:

> The word that came to Jeremiah from the Lord: "Stand in the gate of the Lord's house, and proclaim there this word, and say, Hear the word of the Lord, all you men of Judah who enter these gates to worship the Lord. Thus says the Lord of hosts, the God of Israel, Amend your ways and your doings, and I will let you dwell in this place.

> Do not trust in these deceptive words: 'This is the
> temple of the Lord, the temple of the Lord, the
> temple of the Lord.'
> "For if you truly amend your ways and your do-
> ings, if you truly execute justice one with another,
> if you do not oppress the alien [the stranger], the
> fatherless or the widow, or shed innocent blood in
> this place, and if you do not go after other gods to
> your own hurt, then I will let you dwell in this
> place, in the land that I gave of old to your fathers
> for ever" (Jer. 7:1–7).

In order to understand what had happened at this time,
turn to 2 Chronicles, chapters 34 and 35, to get the
historical background of this moment in Judah. Young
king Josiah, in his attempt to turn this nation back to
God, had just given orders to clean up the temple. The
temple had been turned into a warehouse, a storage place,
and had begun to accumulate a lot of junk, as do our
attics and garages today.

It was during this clean-up operation that the high
priest Hilkiah unearthed the old scroll of the Law, probably of Moses' Book of Deuteronomy. In it they read about
the Passover, and discovered that no one in that nation
had celebrated the Passover since the days of Hezekiah,
a hundred years earlier. So orders were given for a great
celebration of the Passover. Scripture tells us that never
before had there been a Passover in Israel like this one.
This king went all out! He ordered sacrifices according to
the Levitical commandments, and had the priests prepare
themselves to conduct the ceremony.

Den of Robbers

The great day arrived when the sacrifices were to be
offered in the temple. The companies of singers and

chanters were prepared, and the great procession, headed by the king himself, was on its way to the temple to worship there and to obey the command of God to perform the Passover supper. The priests were swinging their incense pots, chanting as they went, and the choir was singing a hymn which included these words: "The temple of the Lord, the temple of the Lord, the temple of the Lord." People were heaving a sigh of relief and thinking, "*Now* God is satisfied. Now he will save us. Now the nations around will not take us over, because at last we are settling our religious accounts with God." And on the way, as they were chanting this chorus, suddenly to everyone's astonishment a young man climbed up to a prominent place on the steps of the temple and yelled out, "HOLD IT!" And everybody stopped. He began to speak:

> "Hear the word of the Lord, all you men of Judah who enter these gates to worship the Lord. Thus says the Lord of hosts, the God of Israel, Amend your ways and your doings, and I will let you dwell in this place. Do not trust in these deceptive words: 'This is the temple of the Lord, the temple of the Lord, the temple of the Lord'" (Jer. 7:2–4).

The gist of his message was, "Whom do you think you're kidding? Do you really think God is like this, that all he is interested in is religious games and rituals? Do you really think that if you merely get all this religion going, God will be fooled and will spare this land? Don't you know that God knows what is going on?" And he went on to describe their actions:

> "Behold, you trust in deceptive words to no avail. Will you steal, murder, commit adultery, swear falsely [commit perjury], burn incense to Baal, and go after other gods that you have not

known, and then come and stand before me in this
house, which is called by my name, and say, 'We
are delivered!'—only to go on doing all these abominations? Has this house, which is called by my
name, become a den of robbers in your eyes?"
(Jer. 7:8–11).

That sounds very much like what happened some centuries later when another young man stood up in the
temple and, fashioning a whip of cords, began to drive
the moneychangers out of the temple, saying, "You have
turned my Father's house into a den of robbers." But here,
Jeremiah has dramatically interrupted the proceedings,
he delivers the message which God has for this people.
They were counting on two things: the fact that the temple was now clean, and the discovery of the Law:

"How can you say, 'We are wise,
    and the law of the Lord is with us'?
But, behold, the false pen of the scribes
    has made it into a lie.
The wise men shall be put to shame,
    they shall be dismayed and taken;
lo, they have rejected the word of the Lord,
    and what wisdom is in them?" (Jer. 8:8–9).

Here is a people who were trusting in performance, in
outward ritual, and they did not realize that God knows
the heart, and that he knew what was going on. Therefore the only thing left to this people was that they be
judged. When people get so blind that they cannot see
what they are doing, and they really think that God cannot see any further than the outward appearance of their
lives, the only thing that will open their eyes is judgment.
So the prophet said these words to them:

"Go now to my place that was in Shiloh [in the Northern kingdom, Israel], where I made my name dwell at first, and see what I did to it for the wickedness of my people Israel. [They had been led into captivity.] And now, because you have done all these things, says the Lord, and when I spoke to you persistently you did not listen, and when I called you, you did not answer, therefore I will do to the house which is called by my name, and in which you trust, and to the place which I gave to you and to your fathers, as I did to Shiloh. And I will cast you out of my sight, as I cast out all your kinsmen, all the offspring of Ephraim" (Jer. 7:12–15).

It was at this point that Jeremiah was told not to pray for this people any longer, for God had decided to visit them with judgment.

Where Is the Healer?

Now, do you think that what God is really saying is, "Look, I've had it! I can't stand this any longer. I'm going to get rid of these people. I'm going to smash them and destroy them. I'm through with them!"? If you do, you have missed what this is all about. But that is evidently what Jeremiah understood God to mean, and as a result he was deeply grieved. He did not understand what God was doing. Chapter 8 gives us the prophet's personal reaction:

> My grief is beyond healing,
>   my heart is sick within me.
> Hark, the cry of the daughter of my people
>   from the length and breadth of the land:
> "Is the Lord not in Zion?
>   Is her King not in her?" (Jer. 8:18–19).

He was looking forward to what was coming—visualizing it, feeling heartsick and anguished, in agony over what was about to happen, especially to the women and the beautiful girls of Judah. It is interesting that in chapter 16 God told this prophet, "I don't want you ever to get married. I don't want you to have a wife and children." So Jeremiah remained unmarried, and he was greatly concerned that these beautiful maidens of Judah would suffer this way. He is crying out on their behalf. And God answers, in verse 19: "Why have they provoked me to anger with their graven images, and with their foreign idols?" But Jeremiah continues his questioning:

"The harvest is past, the summer is ended,
    and we are not saved." [This is the cry of the people.]
For the wound of the daughter of my people is my heart
    wounded,
    I mourn, and dismay has taken hold on me.
Is there no balm in Gilead?
    Is there no physician there?
Why then has the health of the daughter of my people
    not been restored? (Jer. 8:20–22).

Do you see what he is saying? Jeremiah feels so intensely what is going to happen that he cries out, "God, where are you? Where is the healer? Where is the one who can restore this people? Where is the balm in Gilead, the physician who can make a sick person well?" Have you ever felt like that? Have you ever suffered over some loved one, and cried out, "God, where is the Great Physician?" So Jeremiah cries out, "Why don't you heal this people?" He simply doesn't understand what God is doing.

In order to get all this together, we need to look back to chapter 7 and see the list of actions God says he takes when a nation or an individual begins to turn away from him. Verse 13: "And now, because you have done all

these things, says the Lord, and when I spoke to you
persistently you did not listen . . ." The first thing God
does when you begin to drift is to warn you what the
consequences are going to be. He is faithful to tell you
that if you "sow to the flesh you will of the flesh reap
corruption." There is no way to escape it. Even forgiveness for it does not remove that. If you sow to the flesh,
you will of the flesh reap corruption. Sin will leave its
scars even though the wound is healed. God warns that
there is going to be hurt in your life, hurt in your heart,
hurt for the loved ones around you. There is no way to
escape it. But then he says, ". . . and when I called you,
you did not answer . . ." The call of God is a picture of
love seeking a response, reminding you of who he is, and
how much he loves you, trying in various ways to awaken
a response of love and gratitude, to call you back. He is
like the father in the story of the prodigal son, watching
the horizon for that son to return, longing for him to come
back. This is the picture of God, patiently looking after
men and women, boys and girls, being faithful to them,
longing to have them back, calling them again and again.
This may go on for years in the case of an individual.
And all this time he asks us to pray for those like this, to
hold them up, to reach out to them by the power of prayer.

The Last Loving Act

But when that does not work, he has one step left in
the program: judgment. You see, judgment is not God's
way of saying, "I'm through with you." It is not a mark
of the abandonment of God; it is the last loving act of
God to bring you back. It is the last resort of love. C. S.
Lewis put it very beautifully when he said, "God whispers
to us in our pleasures; he speaks to us in our work; he
shouts at us in our pain." Every one of us knows that there

have been times when we would not listen to God, would not pay any attention to what his Word was saying until one day God put us flat on our backs or allowed us to be hurt badly. Then we began to listen. This is what Jeremiah had to learn. He did not understand that this nation had reached the place where the only thing that would heal it, the only chance it had left, was the judgment of God—the hurt and the pain of invasion, and the loss of its national status. God's love insisted that that happen.

Now you can see why he commanded that prayer cease, but that preaching continue. If you read through the Scriptures you see that prayer delays judgment, but preaching hastens it. And what this nation needed to restore it and heal it was judgment. So God said, "Don't delay it; don't hold me back. This is what will do the work. Radical surgery is all that is left, so stop praying." You can see that prayer holds off judgment in the case of Sodom and Gomorrah. Abraham held off the hand of God, steadily reducing the minimum number of righteous men by which that region could be saved, and almost saved the area from the destruction of God. But preaching hastens judgment, because the Word is true. And when truth is revealed to us, and God calls things what they really are, as he does here—adultery, stealing, murder, perjury—instead of accepting the polite names the people themselves were using, and yet they would heed, then judgment is hastened. Jesus said of the Pharisees, "If I had not come and spoken to them, they would not have sin; but now they have no excuse for their sin" (John 15:22). Thus preaching hastens judgment.

It was at this point that Jeremiah broke down and wept before God. I do not think you can read these passages expressing the anguish of the prophet's heart without hearing an echo of the sobs of God. For God was still working through this man, and weeping over this people himself, as expressed in the sobs of Jeremiah. In the midst of Jeremiah's despair, God, in tenderness and beautiful concern, speaks to the prophet and says something to help him:

> Thus says the Lord: "Let not the wise man glory in his wisdom, let not the mighty man glory in his might, let not the rich man glory in his riches; but let him who glories glory in this, that he understands and knows me, that I am the Lord who practice steadfast love, justice, and righteousness in the earth; for in these things I delight, says the Lord" (Jer. 9:23–24).

What a revelation of the greatness of God! Far beyond the greatness of men, a God of wisdom and knowledge is at work. And the prophet's heart was directed to think of that. Man's wisdom is not enough. "Let not the wise man glory in his wisdom . . ." Why not? Well, because man's wisdom is always partial wisdom. It never sees the whole story, never is wide enough to take in all the factors involved. It is tunnel vision, narrow and limited. And that is why we are always thinking we have arrived at solutions to problems only to find in a few years that the "solution" has only made the problem worse. Pollution is a case in point, is it not? And so is warfare, and all the other great problems that confront us today. Man's wisdom is not enough. T. S. Eliot put it so beautifully when he said,

> All our knowledge brings us nearer to our ignorance,
> All our ignorance brings us nearer to death,
> But nearness to death no nearer to GOD
> [Then he asks the question which hangs over this whole
>   generation.]

Where is the Life we have lost in living?*
Where *is* the life we have lost in living? No, you cannot
trust in the wisdom of man, can you?

Nor can you trust in the might of man: ". . . let not
the mighty man glory in his might . . ." Why not? Look
at a man with great power and authority, such as a dicta-
tor, with a great force at his command. Why does he not
have the right to glory? Because his force is directed
only at material things. It has no power to oppose an idea
or a moral value. That is what we learned in those last
few bitter years in Viet Nam, is it not? We thought, at
the end of World War II, that in the atom bomb we had
the most powerful force history had ever known, and we
could be the leading nation in all the world. Who could
oppose us? But atom bombs are no good against ideas.
They can only obliterate people, and 'when they are all
through smashing and destroying, the ideas remain.

No, ". . . let not the mighty man glory in his might,
and let not the rich man glory in his riches . . ." Why
not? Because riches can buy only a very limited number
of things. Jesus spoke of the deceitfulness of riches.
Riches give man a feeling of power that he does not really
have. They give him a feeling of being loved when he
really is not, and of being respected when he is not respected at all. Riches cannot buy love and joy and peace
and harmony.

Cause for Glory

Then what should you glory in? "Ah, glory in this,
Jeremiah, that you know me, and you have available to

From "The Rock" in T. S. Eliot, *The Wasteland and Other
Poems* (New York: Harvest Book, Harcourt, Brace, & World,
1934).

you the wisdom of God. True wisdom is the wisdom of God, and you can correct your own faulty, frail human wisdom with my wisdom. You have the might of God at your disposal, greater than anything the world knows about, a mighty moral force which is irresistible. And you have riches beyond all comparison, the simple riches of love and peace and joy and grace and mercy and truth, which no money can buy. Glory in this, Jeremiah." And so, as the prophet comes to the end of this discourse you find him reflecting on what God has taught him: "I know, O Lord, that the way of man is not in himself, that it is not in man who walks to direct his steps" (Jer. 10: 23). Have you found that out? What a fantastic lesson that is! The way of man is not in himself. It is not in man to direct his steps. You do not have what it takes to live life by yourself. When I was in Minneapolis recently in the midst of a blizzard, I remembered how, thirty-five years ago, I had come through that city for the first time —a young man twenty-one years of age, riding a bus on my way to Chicago and a job I had obtained through correspondence. I had never been to Chicago, having just come out of the plains of Montana, a country boy on the way to the big city. I was inwardly scared to death, uncertain, not knowing where to go or how to react to people, but trying to bluff it through. All the feeling of that time came flooding back, and I remembered that all through the years since then I have felt the hand of God at the critical moments in my life—guiding me, correcting me, rebuking me, setting me straight, changing me, gradually leading me on, opening doors here, closing doors there. I bowed my head in my hotel room and gave thanks that "the way of man is not in himself, that it is not in man who walks to direct his steps," but God will

4

Faith at the Breaking Point

I want to begin this part of our study in the prophecy of Jeremiah by quoting an advertisement that touches upon the preparation needed by God's man in God's age:

> Wanted: A minister for a growing church—a real challenge for the right man. Opportunity to become better acquainted with people. Applicant must offer experience as shop worker, office manager, educator (all levels, including college), artist, salesman, diplomat, writer, theologian, politician, Boy Scout leader, children's worker, minor league athlete, psychologist, vocational counselor, psychiatrist, funeral director, wedding consultant, master of ceremonies, circus clown, missionary, and social worker. Helpful but not essential: experience as a butcher, baker, cowboy, and Western Union messenger. Must know all about the problems of birth, marriage, and death; must also be conversant with latest theories and practices in areas like pediatrics, economics, and nuclear science. Right man will hold firm views on every topic, but is careful not to upset people who disagree. Must be forthright but flexible. Returns

criticism and backbiting with Christian love and forgiveness. Should have outgoing, friendly disposition at all times. Should be a captivating speaker and intent listener. Will pretend he enjoys hearing women talk. Directly responsible for views and conduct to all church members and visitors; not confined to direction or support from any one person. Salary not commensurate with experience or need. No overtime pay. All replies kept confidential. Anyone applying will undergo full investigation to determine his sanity.

Although that may be what is demanded in the ministry today, we ought to set that against the biblical truth which is rapidly coming back into focus—that all of us are in the ministry. All God's people are ministers, wherever they are. According to the gifts God has given you, you are a minister, and in the ministry. Perhaps the central lesson of this book is what happened to Jeremiah as God prepared him to minister in a day of decay. He was called to a strange and difficult ministry. God gradually had to prepare him and toughen him increasingly for the assignments he was to be given in this nation. Jeremiah struggled with his commission. He wept over it, pleaded with God for this people. And the more he wept and pleaded, the harder God seemed to grow, and the more adamant and determined to judge.

In the passage we will examine now, thirteen years have passed in Jeremiah's life since his last message. King Josiah, the last godly king in Judah, had made a valiant effort to try to reform the nation, to overcome its idol worship and to restore the worship of Jehovah. Outwardly the people had gone along with him, but inwardly there was still deep-seated rebellion and revolt. At last, as recounted in 2 Chronicles 35, Josiah met his death when, disobeying the word of God, he went out to do battle with the king of Egypt, Neco, who was on his way to the battle of Carchemish. There on the plain of Megiddo, where the last battle of all the ages will be fought (the battle of Armageddon), king Josiah met his death. He was mourned in Israel, and Jeremiah the prophet made a lamentation for him which is recorded in the Book of Lamentations.

So Jeremiah was plunged into an even more difficult time than he had ever known before. The young son of Josiah, Jehoahaz, came to the throne. But he was a very weak king and within three months had been deposed by the king of Egypt, and his brother, Jehoiakim, was placed on the throne. This was a troubled time in the nation. Around it the great powers of earth, the superpowers of that day, were vying and contending with one another for supremacy in the affairs of the world. Egypt was on its way down, Assyria was melting away, the might of Babylon was looming on the horizon. It was a world of unrest and great turmoil. Judah was caught in the jaws of a nutcracker, situated between the great empires of that day.

Treacherous Friends

In chapter 11 God sends young Jeremiah back to the nation with another word of warning and denunciation. It is very similar to other messages which Jeremiah had to deliver repeatedly to these people—a warning that God would not allow them to get away with their unbelief, their revolt, their violence, and their worship of other gods, and that he was determined to judge them. For the third time now in Jeremiah's ministry, God tells him not to pray for this nation: "Therefore do not pray for this people, or lift up a cry or prayer on their behalf, for I will not listen when they call to me in the time of their trouble" (Jer. 11:14). God had laid a vocal quarantine on Jeremiah, and said, "I do not want you to pray, for prayer delays judgment." What we are going to see now is God's toughening of this young man in preparation for what was coming. Jeremiah was already distressed by God's failure to listen to him, but what was worse, this account tells us, was what he found awaiting him on his return home. In his hometown of Anathoth he learned that his own neighbors and friends had plotted to take his life. He tells us about it, beginning in verse 18:

> The Lord made it known to me and I knew;
>   then thou didst show me their evil deeds.
> But I was like a gentle lamb
>   led to the slaughter.

He suddenly realizes how naïve and blind he had been to trust these neighbors and friends. Now they had plotted against his life.

> I did not know it was against me
>   they devised schemes, saying,
> "Let us destroy the tree with its fruit,
>   let us cut him off from the land of the living,
>   that his name be remembered no more" (Jer. 11:19).

Jeremiah was dismayed that his friends would refuse to support him and would betray him in this way. He comes to the Lord and cries out,

> But, O Lord of hosts, who judgest righteously,
>   who triest the heart and the mind,
> let me see thy vengeance upon them,
>   for to thee have I committed my cause (Jer. 11:20).

He did the right thing. He brought his problem to the Lord. Some of us do not bother to do that when a trial comes upon us; we run to somebody else. But Jeremiah brought it to the Lord. Still, he was a thoroughgoing evangelical, for he also had a complete plan of how God ought to solve it! He wanted God to wreak vengeance upon those who were threatening him, and he expected God to do it. But the Lord told him,

> Therefore thus says the Lord concerning the men of Anathoth, who seek your life, and say, "Do not prophesy in the name of the Lord, or you will die by our hand"—therefore thus says the Lord of hosts: "Behold, I will punish them; the young men shall die by the sword; their sons and their daughters shall die by famine; and none of them shall be left. For I will bring evil upon the men of Anathoth, the year of their punishment" (Jer. 11:21–23).

God says to Jeremiah, "You're right; I will punish these men, but I will do it in my time. They are going to have a part in the judgment which is coming upon Judah. They shall suffer in the famine and in the attack coming from Babylon, but it will be when I say." That is one of the difficult things about dealing with God, is it not? He has his own time schedule. We want him to act now. We say, "Lord, look at the opportunity you've got! It's all set up. And if you'd just do this now, everything would work out." But God ignores us, and says, "I'll do it in my own time." That was one of the hard things Jeremiah had to learn, as it is with every one of us. God does not move on our time schedule, much as we would like him to. In chapter 12 Jeremiah goes on to present his case before the Lord: "Righteous art thou, O Lord, when I complain to thee . . ." (vs. 1). "I know that what you are doing is right, Lord. I know that you cannot do wrong." This, by the way, is a great lesson to learn, for we are sometimes tempted to say, "God is not right; he's wrong!" Jeremiah began the right way. And yet there were great, vexing questions which came into his troubled heart, and he shares them: "Why does the way of the wicked prosper? Why do all who are treacherous thrive?" (Jer. 12:1), and: "How long will the land mourn, and the grass of every field wither?" (Jer. 12:4). I'm sure you recognize these as the standard questions men ask when things begin to go wrong in an individual life, or in the life of a community, or a nation. One time when I was in Fort Worth teaching a Bible class to a group of Young Life youth, I noticed that they seemed rather serious, far more so than usual. I asked what was wrong, and found out that a very well-known and well-liked high school girl in that city had disappeared mysteriously a few days before, and no one knew where she was. All her high school friends were praying for her. She was a Christian, and they were sure that God would protect her.

Harder Times Coming

Just an hour before the class met that night, word had come over the radio that her body had been found. She had been sexually abused and killed. These young people were stunned, and they were asking this same question: "Why? If there's a God of love and power, why couldn't he have done something about it? If he is a God of power, he could act. If he is a God of love, he would want to act. Why does he sit there and let things like this happen?" That is one of the great questions thrown at our faith again and again in this day and age. This is what Jeremiah was crying out to God about. And God's response is very interesting:

"If you have raced with men on foot, and they have wearied
> you,
> how will you compete with horses?
And if in a safe land you fall down,
> how will you do in the jungle of the Jordan?" (Jer. 12:5).

In other words, "Jeremiah, what are you going to do when it gets worse? If this kind of thing throws you, if your faith is challenged and you are upset and you cry out to me and ask these questions, what are you going to do when it gets very much worse? Then where are you going to turn? If you become tired while running with the men on foot, what are you going to do when you have to run against horses? And if in running through the open prairie you fall down, what are you going to do when you have to struggle through a hot, sweaty jungle, whose thick growth impedes your progress at every step?" These are searching questions, are they not?

We are hearing more and more chilling reports about such things as the rise of the occult, and the way demonism and satanism are moving into every level of life in our country today. Famines are already beginning in various parts of the world, just as the "prophets of gloom and doom," as they were called a few years ago, had predicted. A great famine is raging across the central part of Africa, as the Sahara Desert, for no reason known to man, steadily moves southward at the rate of eleven miles a year. Thousands of people are starving to death in the Sudan right now. Jesus said that as we near the end, there will come earthquakes and famines and wars, with nation rising up against nation, and frightening things in the sea—the roaring of the waves—will make men afraid. And he called all this "the beginnings of sorrow," merely the beginnings. "Now, if faith grows cold and faint and weak in the midst of the pressures of today," God's question to Jeremiah, and to us, is, "what are you going to do when it gets worse? How will you compete with horses, when you give in against men on foot?"

Evidently Jeremiah expected God to make things right before they got worse. I think most of us are due for a shock in our Christian lives when we discover that God doesn't always work out our problems on easy terms. That is where Jeremiah is right now. God does not say, "Don't worry, Jeremiah, I'll work out your problems. I'll take care of everything. You won't have any more strain. Go right back to work." He says, "Jeremiah, it's going to get worse, a lot worse; what are you going to do then?" Then he begins to detail some of the things that are in store for him. In fact, he begins with one of the first things Jeremiah was to find when he got home. "If you were disturbed by the fact that your friends and neighbors had betrayed you and were plotting against your life," God says, "listen to this!"

> "For even your brothers and the house of your father,
>   even they have dealt treacherously with you;
>   they are in full cry after you;
> believe them not,
>   though they speak fair words to you" (vs. 6).

"Jeremiah, your own family is part of the plot." What do you think that must have done to Jeremiah? Furthermore, God went on to point out that judgment was absolutely inevitable for this nation. Nothing Jeremiah could do would stop it. In verses 7 and 8, God says,

> "I have forsaken my house,
>   I have abandoned my heritage;

> I have given the beloved of my soul
>   into the hands of her enemies.
> My heritage has become to me
>   like a lion in the forest,
> she has lifted up her voice against me;
>   therefore I hate her."

Now, that is God speaking! "I hate her!" What does it do to your theology when the God of love says, "I hate her—the beloved of my soul, I hate her." What kind of confusing contrast is this? I know you have to look at this in light of what theologians call the "anthropomorphisms" of Scripture, that is, God speaking in terms of man, as though he were a man. For it is true that the inherent nature of God is love, and he can never be anything but a God of love. And yet, love can be so offended and rejected that it acts as though it hates. That is what Jeremiah was facing here. God goes on to describe what he is going to do in the land, and how he will deliver it to judgment. But then there is a word of hope, a ray of light in verses 14 and 15:

> Thus says the Lord concerning all my evil neighbors who touch the heritage which I have given my people Israel to inherit: "Behold, I will pluck them up from their land, and I will pluck up the house of Judah from among them. And after I have plucked them up, I will again have compassion on them, and I will bring them again each to his heritage and each to his land."

The final message of God is not one of hate; it is always one of love and compassion. But in between we have to face the fact that God sometimes does strange things that we cannot understand at the time. This is one of the most challenging issues of the Christian faith. One of the great tests of our faith is when we reach that day when we can no longer understand what God is doing, when it does not seem to be in line with his promises at all. And we have to stand amazed like Paul and say, "Who has known the mind of the Lord, or who has been his counselor? Oh, the depth of the riches both of the wisdom and knowledge of God! How unsearchable are his judgments and his ways past finding out!" (Rom. 11:33–34).

Wear, but Don't Wash!

Well, God is not through with Jeremiah, and in the next chapter we find another one of those amazing visual aids which God employs to teach this young prophet a great and marvelous truth. In chapter 13 Jeremiah is given a sign, and we have to call it "the sign of the dirty shorts"! For, believe it or not, he says,

> Thus said the Lord to me, "Go and buy a linen waistcloth, and put it on your loins [that is, nothing more nor less than a pair of linen shorts], and do not dip it in water" (Jer. 13:1).

Most men nowadays, when they buy underwear, look for the wash-and-wear variety—at least I do. But here God says, "Wear it, but don't wash it." He expected Jeremiah to buy a new pair of linen shorts, to put them on, but not to wash them. What in the world would God be teaching by this? If you skip ahead to verse 11 for a moment, you will see what he is after:

> "For as the waistcloth clings to the loins of a man, so I made the whole house of Israel and the whole house of Judah cling to me, says the Lord, that they might be for me a people, a name, a praise, and a glory, but they would not listen."

In other words, God chose them, designed them, for intimacy. A pair of shorts is the most intimate garment a man can wear, and God uses this wonderful figure to instruct us that this is what he had designed his people for—to be as intimate to him as a pair of shorts would be to a man. I remember the advertisement of an underwear company a number of years ago—you do not see it very often any more. It said, "Next to yourself, you'll love BVDs." That is what God is saying here; next to himself, closest to himself, in the most intimate relationship possible, he wants his people—*in order* that they might be a people, a name, a praise, a glory unto him, a people for his name. He is teaching Jeremiah what his people meant to him, and what he had designed for them, and the glory which was possible to them in the intimacy of a relationship with God.

But now Jeremiah was sent to do something with these shorts:

> So I bought a waistcloth according to the word of the Lord, and put it on my loins. [We do not know how long he wore it, but it evidently got quite dirty, since he was forbidden to wash it.] And the word of the Lord came to me a second time. "Take the waistcloth which you have bought, which is upon your loins, and arise, go to the Euphrates, and hide it there in a cleft of the rock" (Jer. 13: 2–4).

Good for Nothing

The Euphrates River was about two hundred miles away, on the border of Babylon, the nation which would come to bring judgment upon this people. Jeremiah had to journey two hundred miles to the Euphrates River wearing his dirty shorts, hide them in the cleft of a rock, leave them there, and retrace the two hundred miles to Judah. Then he tells us, in verses 6 and 7:

> And after many days the Lord said to me, "Arise, go to the Euphrates, and take from there the waist-cloth which I commanded you to hide there." Then I went to the Euphrates, and dug, and I took the waistcloth from the place where I had hidden it. And behold, the waistcloth was spoiled; it was good for nothing.

You can imagine the shape it was in. It was already dirty when Jeremiah had hidden it there. Exposed to the elements—the rain, the wind, the sun—the cloth would rot and shred. Finally, when Jeremiah came back and dug it out of the cleft of the rock, it was dirty, rotten, shredding, hardly able to hold together, worthless. Standing there with those worthless shorts in his hand, he tells us,

> Then the word of the Lord came to me: "Thus says the Lord: Even so will I spoil the pride of Judah and the great pride of Jerusalem. This evil people, who refuse to hear my words, who stubbornly follow their own heart and have gone after other gods to serve them and worship them, shall be like this waistcloth, which is good for nothing" (vss. 8–10).

Jeremiah was taught how a life begins to rot when it turns away from God. It cannot be sustained in its strength, for God is the source of all strength in humanity. Man cannot be man apart from God. Any individual, or any nation, that refuses to live on this basis, will find his life beginning to rot and to shred, and to lose its power. He will be as this waistcloth—good for nothing.

The rest of the chapter goes on to show how moved and stirred Jeremiah is by this, as he pleads with the people:

> Hear and give ear; be not proud,
>   for the Lord has spoken.
> Give glory to the Lord your God
>   before he brings darkness,
> before your feet stumble
>   on the twilight mountains,
> and while you look for light
>   he turns it into gloom
>   and makes it deep darkness.
> But if you will not listen,
>   my soul will weep in secret for your pride;
> my eyes will weep bitterly and run down with tears,
>   because the Lord's flock has been taken captive
>   (Jer. 13:15–17).

Do you see the effect upon Jeremiah of his own ministry? Then, to make it worse, God sends a severe drought upon the land. In verse 1 of chapter 14, we read, "The word of the Lord which came to Jeremiah concerning the drought . . ." He goes on to describe the land, how the cisterns have no water, the ground is dismayed, there is no rain on the land, the crops are dried up, and wild asses stand and pant, because there is no water in all of the land. This is part of the judging hand of God. Once again this arouses questions in Jeremiah's heart. He says, "Though our iniquities testify against us, act, O Lord, for thy name's sake . . ." Do you see what he is saying? "I understand that you have to judge this people because of their wickedness, Lord, but what about you? You're the healer, you're the God who can restore wicked people. For *your* name's sake, do this."

". . . for our backslidings are many,
   we have sinned against thee.
O thou hope of Israel,
   its savior in time of trouble,
why shouldst thou be like a stranger in the land,
   like a wayfarer who turns aside to tarry for a night?
Why shouldst thou be like a man confused,
   like a mighty man who cannot save?
Yet thou, O Lord, art in the midst of us,
   and we are called by thy name;
      leave us not" (Jer. 14:7–9).

Have you ever come to that place? Many a man of God, in the record of the Scriptures, has turned away the judging hand of God by pleading the glory of God himself. Moses did, Samuel did, and others had stood before God and said, "Regardless of what we're like, God, remember what you're like. Surely, for your own name's sake you won't let this thing happen, lest your name be defiled among the nations." And this is Jeremiah's cry. He is reaching out to God on the highest level of prayer possible, and he closes the chapter with an eloquent plea to God. Consider these words:

Hast thou utterly rejected Judah?
   Dost thy soul loathe Zion?
Why hast thou smitten us
   so that there is no healing for us?
We looked for peace, but no good came;
   for a time of healing, but behold, terror.
We acknowledge our wickedness, O Lord,
   and the iniquity of our fathers,
      for we have sinned against thee
Do not spurn us, for thy name's sake;
   do not dishonor thy glorious throne;
      remember and do not break thy covenant with us.

Are there any among the false gods of the nations that can
> bring rain?
Or can the heavens give showers?
Art thou not he, O Lord our God?
> We set our hope on thee,
> for thou doest all these things (Jer. 14:19–22).

That is great praying, is it not? But look at God's answer:

> Then the Lord said to me, "Though Moses and
> Samuel stood before me, yet my heart would not
> turn toward this people. Send them out of my
> sight, and let them go! And when they ask you,
> 'Where shall we go?' you shall say to them, 'Thus
> says the Lord:
> "Those who are for pestilence, to pestilence,
> > and those who are for the sword, to the sword;
> those who are for famine, to famine,
> > and those who are for captivity, to captiv-
> > ity." (Jer. 15:1–2).

God does not budge an inch. Now, what are you going to
do with a God like that? When God gets that immovable,
it is a great threat to faith. But God is not yet through
with Jeremiah. Though he seems to be adamant and
harsh and unyielding, and goes on to repeat his threats
to the nation, he has something more to say.

Have You Lied to Me, God?

Chapter 15 closes with Jeremiah finally praying for
himself. He has been forbidden to pray for the people,
and so he cries out for himself:

O Lord, thou knowest;
> remember me and visit me,
> and take vengeance for me on my persecutors.

In thy forbearance take me not away;
  know that for thy sake I bear reproach (Jer. 15:15).

Then he thinks back to Josiah's day, when the word of
God was found in the temple, and he says,

Thy words were found, and I ate them,
    and thy words became to me a joy
    and the delight of my heart;
for I am called by thy name,
    O Lord, God of hosts (vs. 16).

But he is wretched, hurt, and despairing, and he cries
out in verse 18,

Why is my pain unceasing,
    my wound incurable,
    refusing to be healed?
Wilt thou be to me like a deceitful brook,
    like waters that fail?

Those are the words of a man who is about to lose his
faith entirely. He says that God just seems to pay no attention, to give no heed, to turn a deaf ear. "I cry out to
him, and I'm on the very verge of wondering if God himself is a liar, and that he will prove false in the end."
Have you been to that stage yet? That is a great test of
faith. One of these days, if you have not yet done so, you
may be standing where Jeremiah stood. But now notice
how tenderly and gently God deals with him:

Therefore thus says the Lord:
"If you return, I will restore you,
    and you shall stand before me.
If you utter what is precious, and not what is worthless,
    you shall be as my mouth.

They shall turn to you,
   but you shall not turn to them.
And I shall make you to this people
   a fortified wall of bronze;
they will fight against you,
   but they shall not prevail over you,
for I am with you
   to save you and deliver you,
                              says the Lord.
I will deliver you out of the hand of the wicked,
   and redeem you from the grasp of the ruthless" (vss. 19–
   21).

God answers his own questions here. He had asked Jeremiah, "What will you do, if you've been wearied by running with the men on foot, when you contend with horses? And if in a safe land you fall down, what will you do in the jungle of the Jordan?" Now his answer is, "Jeremiah, even in those hours when everything else seems to be collapsing, and nothing seems to be dependable, if in that hour you will rest on me, you will find that I will strengthen you and see you through. I am the *only* adequate source of strength in any time of trouble. Any other source will fail you." The arm of flesh will fail. But as we sing in the old hymn,

   When through the deep waters I call you to go,
      the rivers of sorrow shall not overflow . . .
   When through fiery trials your pathway shall lie,
      my grace all sufficient shall be your supply. . . .

"I'll never, never leave you," is God's promise to Jeremiah, and to us in this day, as well. God pours on the pressure sometimes, as you see with Jeremiah—not to destroy us, but to toughen us, to make us ready for what is coming. Surely this is just such an hour in America today. Trials such as this nation has never faced lie before us—shortages, famines, burdens—problems we have never known lie ahead of us. And surely nothing is adequate to meet them but the strength of a living God.

5

To Whom Shall We Go?

In these studies in the Book of Jeremiah we have been watching the death of a nation. The kingdom of Judah has been slowly falling apart under the infection of evil which had spread across the face of this land, from the king down to the common people. It has been heading toward the inevitable climax of the judgment of God— the invasion of the nation and the overthrow of the kingdom. This did not come about suddenly. Jeremiah's ministry lasted for over forty years, and God's patience waited throughout that time for any last-ditch repentance. But the nation persisted in its evil, and eventually the judgment came as the prophet had predicted. Meanwhile, we have been watching God toughening his prophet, preparing him for the increasing deterioration of this nation. Things were getting worse and worse, despite the warnings and the preaching of this faithful man of God.

The passage we come to now, chapters 16 and 17, is in many ways the heart of this prophecy. These two messages, along with those in the two chapters which follow, were delivered toward the close of the reign of Jehoiachim. Jehoiachim was another of the sons of Josiah, and succeeded his brother Jehoahaz to the throne. He reigned for eleven years, and it was during this period that Jeremiah uttered these prophecies.

The section opens with another announcement of God's determination to judge this wicked nation. It sets the stage for the remarkable words which God taught Jeremiah in chapter 17. The first note of his message is one of stringent limitation laid upon the prophet himself. That is, God forbade him to do three specific things. First, he forbade him to get married, as the opening words tell us: "The word of the Lord came to me: 'You shall not take a wife, nor shall you have sons or daughters in this place'" (Jer. 16:1). It was not easy for Jeremiah to be a prophet of God. He did not understand what God was doing. Prophets before him had seen the word of God hit with such intensity and power that people were shaken and turned back to the Lord. But Jeremiah only saw the word fall on seemingly deaf ears, and he was hurt by this, and shaken to the core. He rebelled and turned aside, and even tried to stop preaching for a while (we will see more of that later), but he could not stop.

To Spare Him Sorrow

And now, already a lonely, suffering man, Jeremiah receives this additional restriction from God: he is never to know the joys of a home or children, nor the comfort and companionship of a wife. Now God was not trying to be hard on Jeremiah. In fact, if you read on just a verse or two, you find that it was God's love which prompted him to do this to Jeremiah. His desire was to spare this prophet greater sorrow.

"For thus says the Lord concerning the sons and daughters who are born in this place, and con-

cerning the mothers who bore them and the fathers
who begot them in this land: They shall die of
deadly diseases. They shall not be lamented, nor
shall they be buried; they shall be as dung on the
surface of the ground. They shall perish by the
sword and by famine, and their dead bodies shall
be food for the birds of the air and for the beasts of
the earth" (Jer. 16:3–4).

It was to spare Jeremiah this additional grief that God
forbade him to be married. This reminds us of that word
of Paul's in 1 Corinthians 7, where he says, "Now concerning the unmarried . . . in view of the impending
distress it is well for a person to remain as he is." So God
is saying to Jeremiah, "This is a time when the normal
aspects of life need to be laid aside. The nation is hasten-
ing to its judgment—the hour is approaching, crisis is
coming—and for that reason do not encumber yourself
with unnecessary burdens."

Then God laid two other restrictions on the prophet.
Verse 5:

> "For thus says the Lord: Do not enter the house
> of mourning, or go to lament, or bemoan them; for
> I have taken away my peace from this people, says
> the Lord, my steadfast love and mercy."

And in verses 8 and 9:

> "You shall not go into the house of feasting to sit
> with them, to eat and drink. For thus says the Lord
> of hosts, the God of Israel: Behold, I will make to
> cease from this place, before your eyes and in your
> days, the voice of mirth and the voice of gladness,
> the voice of the bridegroom and the voice of the
> bride."

That is, "There is no time left for the social amenities,
no time for partying or playing games, or even for some

of the usual aspects of life, for time is ripening for judgment, and the end is near." Then, to make it worse, God told Jeremiah, "When you go to this people and announce these words, they will greet them with unbelief, with surprised bewilderment. They will be absolutely appalled at what you say."

> "And when you tell this people all these words, and they say to you, 'Why has the Lord pronounced all this great evil against us? What is our iniquity? What is the sin that we have committed against the Lord our God?' . . ." (vs. 10).

Doctors say that cancer, in its terminal stage, often has a strange way of suddenly seeming to disappear. Many people have been fooled by this. I have known a number of Christians who thought God healed them when they encountered this strange phenomenon. But it only marked the certainty of the end. And here is a nation which is unaware of its evil. It has reached such a degree of sickness that it is no longer aware there is anything wrong at all. And when that happens, it is a sign that the end of the nation is near.

> ". . . then you shall say to them: 'Because your fathers have forsaken me, says the Lord, and have gone after other gods and have served and worshiped them, and have forsaken me and have not kept my law . . .'" (vs. 11).

"You are acting the way you do because you were taught this way. The previous generation had forsaken me," he said. Now, God does not blame them for that. He simply recognizes that this was the case. They had learned wrong ways and wrong attitudes from their parents. But, '. . . you have done worse than your fathers,

for behold, every one of you follows his stubborn evil
will, refusing to listen to me . . .'" (vs. 12). The responsibility they bore for their own judgment was a
refusal to heed what God had said about the evils of
their fathers, and a refusal to turn from their own evil
and come back to God.

In the midst of the darkness God gives a gleam of
hope, promising to restore these people after their exile,
and to bring them back to their own land "which I gave
to their fathers." But in the meantime, the nation is to be
subjected to the ministry of other nations, which will
come like hunters and fishers into the land, robbing it of
all its wealth and treasures.

In verses 19 and 20 we have Jeremiah's amazing response. What would you say if God told you to deliver
such a message today? This is what Jeremiah said:

> O Lord, my strength and my stronghold,
>   my refuge in the day of trouble,
> to thee shall the nations come
>   from the ends of the earth and say:
> "Our fathers have inherited nought but lies,
>   worthless things in which there is no profit.
> Can man make for himself gods?
>   Such are no gods!"

That is what the nations, Jeremiah says, are going to say
to God at last. They are going to come to him and confess the emptiness of all the things they trusted in. Jeremiah lifts up his eyes and looks down the course of the
ages and sees the end of history. And he says, "Lord,
what you're doing now is hard for me to bear; nevertheless, I have a stronghold in you, a place of refuge, and I
know it's going to work! One day the nations are going
to see the result of their incredible folly." And he is

praising God for this. God's response is, "Therefore, behold, I will make them know, this once I will make them know my power and my might, and they shall know that my name is the Lord" (vs. 21). That is, only by the utter collapse of all that men trust in will they ever have their eyes opened to what God has been saying to them. This is why God moves the way he does with individuals—to bring them to the end of themselves, to let them get into trouble and fall apart, and bankrupt themselves in every degree. It is then that both individuals and nations have their eyes opened. Then they see who God is—see his power and his might and his love.

Infectious Evil

So God says that judgment is going to come upon this nation, and they will experience his power—for two reasons. (There should not be a chapter break at this point, for we move right on.) The first reason is that their evil is deeply entrenched:

> "The sin of Judah is written with a pen of iron;
> with a point of diamond it is engraved on the tablet
> of their heart, and on the horns of their al-
> tars . . ." (Jer. 17:1).

Judah's sin is so deeply ingrained in the nation that nothing short of judgment can break it loose. We are facing something similar in our day. We have already seen our nation become deeply entangled with evil. It pervades our government, it runs through our political system and our school system; it invades our homes and recreational life. It is written on the heart with a pen of iron. But, more than that, in Judah's case it was also infectious evil: ". . . their children remember their altars and their Asherim, beside every green tree, and on the high hills, on the mountains in the open country." The next generation was being infected by this, and it could only get worse. Therefore the hand of God must move in judgment. He closes the section by saying,

> "Your wealth and all your treasures I will give for spoil as the price of your sin throughout all your territory. You shall loosen your hand from your heritage which I gave to you, and I will make you serve your enemies in a land which you do not know, for in my anger a fire is kindled which shall burn for ever" (Jer. 17:3–4).

At this point God begins to teach Jeremiah the greatest lessons any man can ever know, the secrets of life. That is why I call the rest of chapter 17 the heart of this whole prophecy. For now God begins to open this young man's eyes to what lies behind the movements of God in history. If you want to understand this day in which we live, and what is happening in this strange, tumultuous, turbulent hour, or the movement of God in the past, you must understand what God now teaches Jeremiah. The first lesson is to show him the two ways by which men can live. And there are only two ways—never both, but one or the other—at any given moment. The first is set forth in verses 5 and 6:

> Thus says the Lord:
> "Cursed is the man who trusts in man
>   and makes flesh his arm,
>   whose heart turns away from the Lord."

Here is a man who trusts in man, who says that man is the ultimate solution to his own problems, and that man is capable of working out all the difficulties of his life and can save himself. God says, "Cursed is that man"; in other words, everything he does will ultimately be brought to nothing. That is what a curse does—it removes the profit, the worth, the value of anything. Look at the symbol God chooses for such a man:

> "He is like a shrub in the desert,
>   and shall not see any good come.
> He shall dwell in the parched places of the wilderness,
>   in an uninhabited salt land."

Walk in the desert and look at the plants there. Notice how wizened and stunted they are. They have great potential, as you can find out by removing them and giving them enough water; then they will grow tremendously. But in the desert they are limited, shrunken, and shriveled. That is a life which trusts in man, either in himself or anybody else.

Planted by Water

In contrast, there is another way man can choose to live: "Blessed is the man who trusts in the Lord, whose trust is the Lord." That is, God himself sustains this man's trust as well as sustaining the man. He keeps his trust alive.

> "He is like a tree planted by water,
>   that sends out its roots by the stream,
> and does not fear when heat comes,
>   for its leaves remain green,
> and is not anxious in the year of drought,
>   for it does not cease to bear fruit" (Jer. 17:8).

In my home state of Montana, in the summer months, we would often have long periods of drought when no rain fell. The land would bake and dry and crack. All the shrubbery would dry up and turn brown and sere. It was a dreary time. But there was one tree down by the stream which always stayed green, no matter how dry the country around became. It was near a hidden, underground spring. No matter what happened elsewhere, that tree remained green and fresh. God says, "The man who has learned to trust in me is like that." He is a man who can take it when things get tough. When everyone else is giving up, he remains inwardly strong, strengthened by a hidden reservoir of strength. This is the secret of a life that trusts in God, and this figure is used frequently in Scripture.

Fatal Heart Disease

In the next two verses you have the heart of the problem and God's solution: "The heart is deceitful above all things, and desperately corrupt . . ." In those two lines you have the explanation of all the misery and heartache and injustice and evil of life. The heart, the natural life into which we were born, has two things wrong with it. First, it is desperately corrupt. This means it never can function as it originally was designed to do. It can never fulfill all your expectations. It will never achieve your ideals nor bring you to the place where you can be what you would like to be. It is corrupt. It is infected with a fatal virus. And it cannot be changed. There is nothing you can do about it, ultimately; it is useless and wasted. Therefore there is only one thing it is good for—to be put to death. And that is exactly what the Lord Jesus Christ did with it when he died some centuries later. He took the fatal nature, human nature, and put it to death, because that was all it was good for.

I know that many people have trouble at this point. This is the verse, among others like it in the Scriptures, which divides humanity right down the center. You either believe this verse, and live the rest of your life on these terms, understanding this fact, or you deny it and say, "It is not true; man is basically good." You have to be on one side or the other. Your whole system of philosophy, education, legislation, and everything else, will be determined by which one of those views you take. This is the Great Divide of mankind.

One of the greatest confirmations of the truth of this verse is the Constitution of the United States of America. Our founding fathers were certainly aware of this great fact—that man, by nature, is desperately corrupt—so that they never trusted a single man, even the best, with ultimate power. They set up checks and balances by which the power of *any* man in office, even the most admired of men, would be scrutinized and examined by others. They did not trust anybody, and rightfully so! I have often quoted these words from Winston Churchill, an astute observer of life:

> Certain it is that, while men are gathering knowledge and power with ever-increasing speed, their virtues and their wisdom have not shown any notable improvement as the centuries have rolled. Under sufficient stress—starvation, terror, warlike passion, or even cold intellectual frenzy—the modern man we know so well will do the most terrible deeds, and his modern woman will back him up.

Churchill understood this verse: "The heart is deceitful above all things, and desperately corrupt." No system of philosophy, of psychology, of education, will ever serve to eliminate the wrongful, evil failing of the human heart. It cannot be done. We have to face life on those terms.

As if it were not bad enough that we have this poisoned well within us, there is also another quality about the heart of man: it is deceitful above all things. It is corrupt but it never looks corrupt. It has an amazing power to disguise itself and look good and hopeful and fair—admirable, even. That is what is so deceitful about it. This explains why, all through the centuries, men continually keep trying to improve human nature. It always looks as if success is only a few steps away, and then man will be perfect. But the approaches men employ are equivalent to trying to improve a poisoned well by painting the pump!

Have you ever felt this way about yourself? "I really am only a few steps short of perfection. I know there are a few little things that I do (and they're always little things, not very significant), just a few minor aberrations, and if I could just correct those, I would be a splendid person to live with!" Do you feel that way? Then you are suffering from the deceitfulness of the heart. It can look good—it has that ability to do so—but it is unable to help itself. It is deceitful above all things.

The heart is crafty, and often hypocritical. Every once in a while we know this about ourselves, don't we? We know that we have a frightening ability to hide a hateful heart under flattering words, or that we can speak softly and lovingly to someone whom we utterly despise. We *know* we can do it; we do it all the time. We can use a sweet tone, and act and sound as if we are perfectly at ease, when inwardly we are seething with revolt and rebellion. That is the heart. It has that ability. It can appear fair. It can make the most impressive vows to do better. It can promise reform, and suffer hardship. Paul says that you can bestow all your goods to feed the poor, without love. You can give your body to be burned, without love, and to do so is worth nothing. No matter how sincere, all these efforts are like a house built upon the sand, doomed to disaster.

The only book in the world that tells you about the heart is the Bible—and those which are based upon it. You will never find that information in any other source. Secular studies of humanity won't lead you to this revelation. This is God himself, opening up a truth which divides the world, and which men *must* know if they are going to face life the way it really is. No wonder Jeremiah's response is one line: ". . . who can understand it?" "Lord, if this is true, how do you expect me to run my own life? How do you expect me to solve my problems? I can't even recognize that I have problems! How do you expect me to know what to do? How can you lay upon me any responsibility, if this is true?" Look at God's solution, verse 10:

> "I the Lord search the mind
>   and try the heart,
> to give to every man according to his ways,
>   according to the fruit of his doings."

You say you want to know what is in your heart? Then look at what comes out in your life. God is at work to make us *act* the way we actually *are*. In chapter 6 of the Book of Galatians, Paul gives us the equivalent of this:

> ". . . for whatever a man sows, that he will also reap. For he who sows to his own flesh [the heart which is evil] will from the flesh reap corruption [because that heart is desperately corrupt]; but he

who sows to the Spirit [the new Spirit from God, given to him in Jesus Christ] will from the Spirit reap eternal life [because that God is a living God]" (vs. 7).

Somewhere Else to Go

The well will produce water according to its nature; the tree will produce fruit according to its nature. The Lord Jesus himself taught us that. Jeremiah's answer to this is beautiful:

Like the partridge that gathers a brood which she did not hatch,
so is he who gets riches but not by right;
in the midst of his days they will leave him,
and at his end he will be a fool (Jer. 17:11).

He is saying that it is useless to count on natural wisdom or natural goodness to enrich your life. If all this is true, then to count on a heart which is desperately corrupt and deceitful above all things, is an absolutely stupid and foolish thing to do! And if you build your life—gain your wealth and value and riches—on that basis, in the midst of your life they will abandon you and leave you desolate. But on the other hand, "A glorious throne set on high from the beginning is the place of our sanctuary" (vs. 12). There is where a man finds the answer to his life, the solution to his problems, the understanding of his own nature, and the supply of his need for a sanctuary, a place to go. One of the reasons men fight the idea that we are born with an evil nature is that they do not know where else to go. To say they have to abandon the only nature they know seems to them to be tantamount to saying, "You have to commit some kind of moral suicide; you have to give your *self* up." People resist that idea, but that, amazingly, is exactly what the gospel says. The good news is that *God* has found a way by which you can die without dying! Isn't that interesting? You can let that old man go, painful and hurtful as it might seem at the time, because you have somewhere else to go—and that place is God himself, the life of God, available in Jesus Christ. "A glorious throne set on high from the beginning"—authority and life—"is the place of our sanctuary." There is where we hide.

The gospel is in the Old Testament as well as in the New, and these old prophets understood this just as much as we do. Here is Jeremiah's lesson. He stands and prays, and his prayer is beautiful: "Heal me, O Lord, and I shall be healed; save me, and I shall be saved . . ." (vs. 14). "No one else can do it. Only the One who sits on a glorious throne set on high from the beginning can heal me." The prophet stands before him and says, "Lord, here I am with this heart which was given to me by birth, which is desperately corrupt, and deceitful above all things. All I can do is bring it to you again and again, Lord, whenever it raises its head, and say, 'Heal me, O Lord, and I shall be healed; save me, and I shall be saved.' "

Whenever the flesh seeks control, whenever false confidence rises within us and says, "Just watch my steam! I'll show them what I can do! Give me a chance; I've got what it takes to handle it!" that is our deceitful heart talking to us. And whenever that occurs, the prophet's advice is, "Run to God, hide in the sanctuary of the glorious throne set on high, where you are seated with Christ in heavenly places." And you will find a place to stand, a resource to live from, and God himself will heal you, and you will be healed; he will save you, and you will be saved.

Bring In No Burden

With that truth under his belt, Jeremiah was sent back to the nation with another message, which closes this chapter. This message is quite different from the first one, so let's look at just a few verses of it:

> Thus said the Lord to me: "Go and stand in the Benjamin Gate, by which the kings of Judah enter and by which they go out, and in all the gates of Jerusalem, and say: 'Hear the word of the Lord, you kings of Judah, and all Judah, and all the inhabitants of Jerusalem, who enter by these gates. Thus says the Lord: Take heed for the sake of your lives, and do not bear a burden on the sabbath day or bring it in by the gates of Jerusalem. And do not carry a burden out of your houses on the sabbath or do any work, but keep the sabbath day holy, as I commanded your fathers' " (Jer. 17: 19–22).

What a strange message to send! Why is God so concerned about the sabbath all through the Bible, from beginning to end, and especially here in the last days of this nation? Why does he focus insistently on the sabbath? He says,

> " 'But if you listen to me, says the Lord, and bring in no burden by the gates of this city on the sabbath day, but keep the sabbath day holy and do no work on it, then there shall enter by the gates of this city kings who sit on the throne of David, riding in chariots and on horses, they and their

princes, the men of Judah and the inhabitants of Jerusalem; and this city shall be inhabited for ever. And people shall come from the cities of Judah and the places round about Jerusalem, from the land of Benjamin, from the Shephelah, from the hill country, and from the Negeb, bringing burnt offerings and sacrifices, cereal offerings and frankincense, and bringing thank offerings to the house of the Lord. But if you do not listen to me, to keep the sabbath day holy . . . then I will kindle a fire in its gates, and it shall devour the palaces of Jerusalem and shall not be quenched' " (vss. 24–27).

Now, what is so important about the sabbath? It is amazing how this message about the sabbath has been distorted in the understanding of men in the church through the ages. The sabbath, you remember, began when God ceased from the work of creation and rested on the seventh day. He ceased from all his works. And he tells man all through the Scriptures that this is a picture of the life of faith and trust in him. You are to cease from your own works and trust in God to work on your behalf. That is keeping the sabbath. All the ceremonials and rituals which gathered around this day are only to illustrate God's point. In the Book of Hebrews he says, ". . . for whoever enters God's rest also ceases from his labors as God did from his" (Heb. 4:10).

The sabbath is a picture to us of how God intends man to live—not by trusting in himself, not by trusting in any other man, or in what other men can do; but accepting this new way of life, which is God himself working in us, God himself living in us. Living by God's design is to make our humanity available to him, with our mind, our emotions, our will, and everything about us, and say,

"Lord, here I am. Here's the situation in front of me, the thing I have to do. (Maybe it is my work tomorrow and all through the week. Maybe it is some special demand made upon me by my children, by my husband or my wife. Maybe it is some difficult situation to which I must respond.) Lord, how do I meet it? Well, here I am, Lord. You meet it in me. I'll do what is necessary, but I'll count on you to do it in me, and you'll be responsible for the results."

That is the sabbath. That means you are at rest inside, because the strain is not on you, it is on God. You are at peace inside because you do not have to be responsible for what happens; he does. That is to approach life at rest. That is the man who never turns dry and barren and sere, but who remains green and strong and fresh in the midst of all the drought and disaster around him. That is the man or woman who remains as a green tree in the time of drought, who stands continually before God in the face of every demand and says, "Heal me, O Lord, and I shall be healed; save me, and I shall be saved."

6

The Potter and the Clay

In chapter 17 we saw that Jeremiah was taught two great truths: "The heart is deceitful above all things, and desperately corrupt." That is, there is no hope in man. But Jeremiah was also shown "a glorious throne set on high from the beginning," which, he tells us, is the place of our sanctuary. There *is* hope in God—the present availability of God to an individual or a nation. And when that person, or that people, turns to God, healing begins to come back. This is in line with the well-known promise of 2 Chronicles 7:14: ". . . if my people who are called by my name humble themselves, and pray and seek my face, and turn from their wicked ways, then I will hear from heaven, and will forgive their sin and heal their land."

In chapter 18 the prophet is taught still another lesson. The chapter opens,

> The word that came to Jeremiah from the Lord: "Arise, and go down to the potter's house, and there I will let you hear my words." So I went down to the potter's house, and there he was work-

ing at his wheel. And the vessel he was making of
clay was spoiled in the potter's hand, and he re-
worked it into another vessel, as it seemed good to
the potter to do (Jer. 18:1–4).

At the potter's house Jeremiah saw three simple things,
which conveyed to him a fantastic lesson. If you were to
go to a potter's shed today, to watch the potter making
vessels of clay, you would observe the same things that
Jeremiah did, for the art of making a pot has not changed
through the centuries. The wheel is now turned by an
electric motor, but even this is still controlled by the foot
of the potter. The clay is the same as it has always been.
The potter is the same, with his capable hands, guided by
his intelligence, working to mold and shape the clay
into the vessel he has in mind.

The Basic Ingredients

When I was in Israel a few years ago, visiting the tomb
of Abraham in the village of Hebron, there was a potter's
house right across the street. I went "down to the potter's house," and there was the potter making his vessel
in the ancient way, unchanged from the days of Jeremiah. There were the same ingredients—the potter, the
clay, and the wheel.

What did Jeremiah see in this lesson? First there was
the clay. Jeremiah knew, as he watched the potter shaping and molding the clay, that he was looking at a picture
of himself, and of every man, and of every nation. We are
the clay. Both Isaiah and Zechariah in the Old Testament
join with Jeremiah in presenting this picture of the potter and the clay. And in the New Testament the voice of
Paul in that great passage in Romans 9 reminds us that
God is the Potter and we are the clay. So Jeremiah saw

the clay being shaped and molded into a vessel. Then some imperfection in the clay spoiled it in the potter's hand, and the potter crumbled it up, and began anew the process of shaping it into a vessel that pleased him.

Jeremiah saw the wheel turning constantly, bringing the clay against the potter's hand. That wheel is life itself under the control of the Potter, for it is the potter's foot that guides the wheel. The circumstances each day brings are the hands of the Potter pressing against the clay of our lives. The lesson is clear. As our life is being shaped and molded by the Great Potter, it is what Browning called "this dance of plastic circumstance," which bring us again and again under the potter's hand, under the pressure of the molding fingers of the Potter, so that he may shape the vessel according to his will.

Then, Jeremiah saw the potter. God, he knew, was the Great Potter, with absolute right over the clay to make it what he wanted it to be. In Romans, Paul argues, "Will what is molded say to its molder, 'Why have you made me thus?' Has the potter no right over the clay, to make out of the same lump one vessel for beauty and another for menial use?" (Rom. 9:20–21) Of course he has such a right. The vessel is shaped according to the image in the potter's mind.

Jeremiah, as he watched, learned that an individual or a nation is clay in the Great Potter's hands. He has a sovereign right to make it what he wants it to be. And if there be some imperfection in the clay, something which mars the design or spoils the work, the potter simply crushes the clay down to a lump and begins once more to make a vessel according to his own mind.

In the verses which follow, this lesson is applied to the nation:

Then the word of the Lord came to me: "O house of Israel, can I not do with you as this potter has done? says the Lord. Behold, like the clay in the potter's hand, so are you in my hand, O house of Israel. If at any time I declare concerning a nation or a kingdom, that I will pluck up and break down and destroy it, and if that nation, concerning which I have spoken, turns from its evil, I will repent of the evil that I intended to do to it. And if at any time I declare concerning a nation or a kingdom that I will build and plant it, and if it does evil in my sight, not listening to my voice, then I will repent of the good which I had intended to do to it" (Jer. 18:5–10).

In more direct terms, the same lesson Jeremiah learned at the potter's house is applied here to the nation. The nation was warned that if it refused to turn from its evil ways (as if the clay were to resist the potter's shaping pressure), then it would be plucked up and destroyed (as the potter crushes what has been spoiled, making it a useless lump of clay once more). The crushing blow God would deal the nation, however, was to issue in restoration, a rebuilding and reshaping of Israel to conform to God's design.

In our own lives, as individuals in Christ, God deals with us in the same way he dealt with the nation of Israel. For us, both God's work with Israel and the potter's work with clay are pictures drawn to help us understand the meaning of the various pressures, trials and even catastrophes that befall us. The wheel of life brings us into contact with the shaping of circumstances, which we need to see as God's hand working to form us into the very person he has in mind. If we resist his pressure, and rebel against the circumstances he allows to come into our lives, that resistance will be crushed. That is what the judgment of Israel and Judah picture for us—not final, ultimate destruction, but a putting to death of the flesh, since it is out of the flesh that we resist God. This process goes on, in big and little steps, throughout our lives to make us truly in the likeness of God.

God Heaves a Sigh

There is a beautiful lesson here also, in the word *repent* as it is used in reference to God. When you and I talk about repenting, we speak in terms of changing our mind. We start out to do something, but circumstances occur which cause us to change our mind, so we do something else. But that is not the way the word is used concerning God. Many Scriptures tell us that God never changes his mind. Although God may appear to have changed his mind, the word *repent* does not adequately express the thought here. The Hebrew word used here means literally, "to heave a sigh." It can be either a sigh of sorrow, or a sigh of relief; the word is used both ways in this passage. God says, "If I say to a nation, 'I'm going to destroy you,' or to an individual, 'I'm going to uproot you and crush you,' and I bring pressure upon you to that end—if you yield to it, if you conform to what the pressure is driving you to, then I will heave a sigh of relief."

Do you remember the days of the Cuban missile crisis, when we learned that the Soviet government was installing missiles in Cuba that were aimed at the hearts of American cities? President Kennedy reacted immediately by ordering the navy to quarantine any missile-carrying ships, threatening to search them if they continued on their courses, which would have been an outright act of war. The nation trembled in uncertainty, wondering if we would be engulfed by a nuclear war with Russia. How tense those days were! And remember how, from every home in this country, there came a collective sigh of relief when it was announced that the Soviets had capitulated. We stood eyeball to eyeball, and they blinked first, as President Kennedy put it, and they removed the missiles from Cuba.

That is the kind of sigh God sighs. It is in that way that he repents. He has one thing in mind—to make a vessel according to his design—and nothing will stop him. But he does not like to judge. He does not like harshness and severity and chastisement. In fact, in the Book of Lamentations, Jeremiah says that God does not willingly afflict the sons of men. He takes no delight in it at all. Isaiah calls judgment "God's strange work." It is not according to the desire of his heart. What he is doing is bringing pressure, molding and shaping the clay, forcing it up and out and into the shape of the vessel he wants it to be, hoping the clay will conform. And when it yields to his touch, he breathes a sigh of relief.

But there is also the sigh of sorrow, as you see occurring here in Judah:

> "Now, therefore, say to the men of Judah and the inhabitants of Jerusalem: 'Thus says the Lord, Behold, I am shaping evil against you and devising a plan against you. [There are the molding fingers of the potter at work.] Return, every one from his evil way, and amend your ways and your doings'" (Jer. 18:11).

There is the heart of the potter, hoping that the pressure he is exerting will be enough so that he can sigh with relief as the clay yields to his hands. But as verse 12 makes clear, in Judah's case it did not happen: "But they say, 'That is in vain! [Forget it, God!] We will follow our own plans, and will every one act according to the stubbornness of his evil heart.' " And so God sighed with sorrow. He expressed it in the verses which follow:

"Therefore thus says the Lord:
Ask among the nations,
    who has heard the like of this?
The virgin Israel
    has done a very horrible thing.
Does the snow of Lebanon leave
    the crags of Sirion?
Do the mountain waters run dry,
    the cold flowing streams?"

Does this ever happen in nature? Does snow melt away from the tops of the high mountains? Yes! Do the waters of these streams ever run dry when the snow is continually melting? No, it is absolutely contrary to nature.

"But my people have forgotten me,
    they burn incense to false gods;
they have stumbled in their ways,
    in the ancient roads,
and have gone into bypaths,
    not the highway,
making their land a horror,
    a thing to be hissed at for ever [literally, a thing
        to be "whistled" at, in amazed dismay].
Every one who passes by it is horrified
    and shakes his head.
Like the east wind I will scatter them
    before the enemy.
I will show them my back, not my face,
    in the day of their calamity" (Jer. 18:13–17).

That is the Potter, sighing with sorrow and smashing the clay down into a lump again, that he might begin anew and make it yet a vessel according to his own design.

Plots Against the Prophet

In verse 18 a very personal note is suddenly interjected. Evidently the king and the government of Judah are upset at the message of Jeremiah. They do not like this proclamation of sudden and certain doom, so they decide to take action against him:

> Then they said, "Come, let us make plots against Jeremiah, for the law shall not perish from the priest, nor counsel from the wise, nor the word from the prophet. Come, let us smite him with the tongue, and let us not heed any of his words."

In other words, the government, from the king down, began to plot against Jeremiah. They said to themselves, "We want to make one thing perfectly clear: This man is not going to change anything in this country. The law shall not perish from the priest, nor counsel from the wise, nor the word from the prophet. In all three branches of government—legislative, executive, and judicial—there will be no change. Nothing is going to happen because of this man. No recession, no problem will come into the land."

Then they launched a campaign of defilement and defamation against Jeremiah. They conspired together to undermine his authority and to speak against him as a person. Undoubtedly, they found ways to secure personal information about him which they could twist so as to defame him. This drove Jeremiah back to the Lord in prayer. He ran to God—the right place to go—but consider this prayer:

Give heed to me, O Lord,
   and hearken to my plea.
Is evil a recompense for good?
   Yet they have dug a pit for my life.
Remember how I stood before thee
   to speak good for them,
   to turn away thy wrath from them.

He reminds God how faithful he had been to intercede for these people, this very nation, how he had pled with God to turn his wrath away from them and spare them. And all he gets for his pains is a campaign of defilement and defamation against him, and a plot against his life. Look how Jeremiah takes it:

Therefore deliver up their children to famine;
   give them over to the power of the sword,
let their wives become childless and widowed.
   May their men meet death by pestilence,
   their youths be slain by the sword in battle.
May a cry be heard from their houses,
   when thou bringest the marauder suddenly upon them!
For they have dug a pit to take me,
   and laid snares for my feet.
Yet, thou, O Lord, knowest
   all their plotting to slay me.
Forgive not their iniquity,
   nor blot out their sin from thy sight.
Let them be overthrown before thee;
   deal with them in the time of thine anger (Jer. 18:19–23).

"Get 'em, Lord!" Isn't that amazing? He could weep before God and pray for these people, intercede for them—as long as he was not personally involved. But when they began aiming at *his* life, then it was a different story.

See what a "good evangelical" Jeremiah was?! "I love humanity; it's people I can't stand!"

Now, Jeremiah's reaction certainly doesn't surprise us. It is simply a confirmation of what Jeremiah learned about himself in chapter 17: "The heart is deceitful above all things, and desperately corrupt." Even a prophet's heart can give way to the temptations of the flesh. Rather than following his Lord and praying, "Father, forgive them, for they know not what they do," Jeremiah's cry is, "Wipe them out, Lord. They're after me, now. Lord, pay 'em back in full measure, in kind!" Well, that is the way we pray, sometimes, and this man is of like passions with us. One of the most instructive things in this book is to see how this mighty prophet, who fulfilled a faithful ministry to this nation, had his times of weakness and trembling, of fear and reaction in the flesh, as this prayer makes clear.

Now God sends Jeremiah back again to the potter's house:

> Thus said the Lord, "Go, buy a potter's earthen flask, and take some of the elders of the people and some of the senior priests, and go out to the valley of the son of Hinnom at the entry of the Potsherd Gate, and proclaim there the words that I tell you" (Jer. 19:1–2).

Back to the potter's house he went, this time not to watch the formation of a vessel in the hands of the potter, but to buy a potter's flask, a vessel already fired in the kiln, hardened, brittle. He was to take it outside the gates of the southern part of Jerusalem to the valley of Hinnom, which is called, in the New Testament, the valley of Gehenna. This was the garbage dump of Jerusalem, the place they threw all the refuse from the streets of the city. All the bodies of dogs and cats and other animals that died in the streets were left there to rot. It was the place where bodies of criminals were thrown after execution, to rot in the sun and be food for vultures—an evil, stinking place. There Jeremiah was to take the elders of the people and some of the senior priests and say these words to them:

> " 'Hear the word of the Lord, O kings of Judah and inhabitants of Jerusalem. Thus says the Lord of hosts, the God of Israel, Behold, I am bringing such evil upon this place that the ears of every one who hears of it will tingle. Because the people have forsaken me, and have profaned this place by burning incense in it to other gods whom neither they nor their fathers nor the kings of Judah have known; and because they have filled this place with the blood of innocents [they had erected altars to the god Molech, a fearsome, grinning god inside of which was built a great fire, and through whose mouth the people passed their living children to be burned alive], and have built the high places of Baal to burn their sons in the fire as burnt offerings to Baal, which I did not command or decree, nor did it come into my mind; therefore, behold, days are coming, says the Lord, when this place shall no more be called Topheth, or the valley of the son of Hinnom, but the valley of Slaughter. And in this place I will make void the plans of Judah and Jerusalem . . .' " (Jer. 19:3–7).

There is the sovereignty of the Potter over the clay. Men make plans, but God makes other plans. Napoleon had to learn that lesson; he once said, "God is on the side of the army with the heaviest artillery." But there came a time in his life when, exiled on the island of St. Helena, he said, "Man proposes; but God disposes."

> " 'And in this place I will make void the plans of Judah and Jerusalem, and will cause their people to fall by the sword before their enemies, and by the hand of those who seek their life. I will give their dead bodies for food to the birds of the air and to the beasts of the earth. And I will make this city a horror, a thing to be hissed [whistled] at; every one who passes by it will be horrified and will hiss because of all its disasters. And I will make them eat the flesh of their sons and their daughters, and every one shall eat the flesh of his neighbor in the siege and in the distress, with which their enemies and those who seek their life afflict them' " (vss. 7-9).

These words came literally true. In only a few years the armies of Nebuchadnezzar surrounded this city, and laid siege to it. The resulting famine grew so severe, as we will see in this very prophecy, that the people resorted to cannibalism and killed and ate their own children, and one another, in order to live. Then the armies broke down the walls of the city and leveled them to the ground, so that later those passing by would whistle in amazement at the destruction which came upon this city.

Now Jeremiah was told to do something with the flask.

> "Then you shall break the flask in the sight of the men who go with you, and shall say to them, 'Thus says the Lord of hosts: So will I break this people and this city, as one breaks a potter's vessel, so that it can never be mended. Men shall bury in Topheth because there will be no place else to bury. Thus will I do to this place, says the Lord, and to its inhabitants, making this city like

Topheth. The houses of Jerusalem and the houses of the kings of Judah—all the houses upon whose roofs incense has been burned to all the host of heaven, and drink offerings have been poured out to other gods—shall be defiled like the place of Topheth'" (vss. 10–13).

Jeremiah was told, in the striking figure God employed for the benefit of these people, to take the potter's vessel he had bought and dash it to pieces on a rock. And as they watched it fly into smithereens, so that it was impossible to bring it back together, these people were taught that they were dealing with a God whose love is so intense that he will *never* alter his purpose—even if he has to destroy and crush and break them down again.

It is that work of God that the world sees right now. They see the hell which is coming into our nation, at every level. And soon it will be worse, according to the prophetic Scriptures. Harder things will happen, and affairs among men will grow worse, until "men's hearts will fail them for fear of seeing the things which are coming to pass on the face of the earth." They will cry out against God as being harsh and ruthless and vindictive, filled with vengeance and anger and hatred. That is all the world sees.

Shaped in Love

But the people of God are taught further truth. Jeremiah had been to the potter's house. He had seen the potter making a vessel, and he knew that it was love behind the Potter's pressures, and that when the vessel was marred, the Potter was capable of crushing it down again, bringing it to nothing but a lump. And then he would mold it, shaping it once again, perhaps many times, until at last it fulfilled what the Potter wanted. That is the great lesson Jeremiah learned at the potter's house, and that we can learn at the potter's house, as well. In Paul's second letter to Timothy he says,

> In a great house there are not only vessels of gold and silver but also of wood and earthenware, and some for noble use, some for ignoble. If any one purifies himself from what is ignoble [those practices which appear just before this in the context—wrongful attitudes, contentiousness, ungodliness, doctrinal aberrations, iniquity] then he will be a vessel for noble use, consecrated and useful to the master of the house, ready for any good work (2 Tim. 2:20–21).

When we are in the Potter's hands, feeling his pressures, feeling the molding of his fingers, we can relax and trust him, for we know that this Potter has suffered with us and knows how we feel, but is determined to make us into a vessel "meet for the master's use." What a tremendous lesson, what a beautiful lesson Jeremiah learned at the potter's house—one which I hope will guide us and guard us under the pressures which are coming into our lives these days. Remember that the Potter has a purpose in mind, and the skill and ability to fulfill it, no matter how many times he may have to make the vessel over again.

7

A Burning in the Bones

Jeremiah's first actual encounter with physical attack
came in the fourth year of the reign of Jehoiakim the
king, when Nebuchadnezzar was on his way to Jerusalem. The armies of Babylon were already marching.
The king had heard of the approach of the Babylonians,
fear had gripped the hearts of the people and of the king
himself, and Jeremiah was sent by God to give a final
word of warning before the judgment actually fell. What
a testimony this book is to the patience of God! For by
now the prophet has been conveying this message for
twenty-two years, and still the judgment has been held
off. But now it is about to come at last, as the nation remains obdurate and stubbornly unrepentant. Chapter 20
should begin with verse 14 of chapter 19:

> Then Jeremiah came from Topheth, where the
> Lord had sent him to prophesy, and he stood in the
> court of the Lord's house, and said to all the peo-
> ple: "Thus says the Lord of hosts, the God of
> Israel, Behold, I am bringing upon this city and
> upon all its towns all the evil that I have pro-

nounced against it, because they have stiffened
their neck, refusing to hear my words."

Now Pashhur the priest, the son of Immer, who
was chief officer in the house of the Lord, heard
Jeremiah prophesying these things. Then Pashhur
beat Jeremiah the prophet, and put him in the
stocks that were in the upper Benjamin Gate of the
house of the Lord (Jer. 19:14–20:2).

Now he was in the stocks! For saying what he had been
saying all along, he suddenly finds himself with his back
bleeding and raw and sore, his arms and legs imprisoned
in stocks which held him in a most uncomfortable position, facing a long, dark, cold, lonely night. By this time
Jeremiah was accustomed to assassination threats. But
this was an official action taken by the chief officer of the
temple, and it indicates how the opposition to the prophet
was hardening at this time.

Between Faith and Despair

I want to skip forward now to verse 7, because beginning here, in poetic form, we have the thoughts of Jeremiah while he is in the stocks, waiting for what would
happen on the morrow. He was, to say the least, a pro-
foundly perturbed prophet! Here we get another look at
the honest humanity of this man, at the way he faced circumstances just as we do, with fear and despair, alternat-
ing at times with faith and confidence. If you have ever
found yourself in unexpected trouble for doing the right
thing, you will be able to identify with Jeremiah at this
time, as he fluctuates between bitterness and faith, between despair and praise. Let us look at the prophet's
dilemma. The first thing he feels is that God himself has
deceived him:

> O Lord, thou hast deceived me,
>   and I was deceived;
> thou art stronger than I,
>   and thou hast prevailed.

Here is a bitter cry. Jeremiah actually charges God with having lied to him, and with having taken advantage of him because he is bigger. Have you ever felt like that toward God? Jeremiah is probably thinking back to the promise with which he began his ministry, recorded in the first chapter. God had called Jeremiah as a young man and set him to his task, and Jeremiah had objected:

> But the Lord said to me,
>   "Do not say, 'I am only a youth';
>   for to all to whom I send you you shall go,
>   and whatever I command you you shall speak.
>   Be not afraid of them,
>   for I am with you to deliver you,
>   says the Lord."
> Then the Lord put forth his hand and touched my
> mouth; and the Lord said to me,
>   "Behold, I have put my words in your mouth.
>   See, I have set you this day over nations and
>   over kingdoms,
>   to pluck up and to break down,
>   to destroy and to overthrow,
>   to build and to plant" (Jer. 1:7–10).

Jeremiah, remembering those words, is saying, "What happened, Lord? What happened to your promise? You said you'd be with me to deliver me, but here I am in these miserable stocks, held a prisoner, my back bloody and sore, and they're threatening my life. You said you'd deliver me! Lord, you've deceived me!"

That is the way the heart can easily feel toward God,

isn't it? Like so many of us, Jeremiah took these promises rather superficially, and he made certain assumptions God never intended. He assumed that "to deliver" meant "to keep him from hurt." But God did not say that. Jeremiah saw himself in rather heroic terms, and though he shrank from that call, he foresaw no pain or personal injury connected with his ministry. He saw himself as going and declaring the word of God to a people who needed it, expecting God to set a wall about him, giving his angels charge over him, keeping him safe through it all. But now he seems to have absolutely no protection, and so he charges God with lying.

Lying, of course, is the one thing God cannot do. There is no way he can be faithless to his promise. And yet Jeremiah feels, as many of us have felt, that God has failed his promise. I do not know how many times people have said to me, referring to the Word of God, "Well, I know what it *says*, but it doesn't work!" That is just another way of saying, "God has deceived me; God's a liar!" And that was the prophet's predicament.

The second thing he found was that people were mocking him: "I have become a laughingstock all the day; every one mocks me." His message was unpopular. And since the people could not answer the keenness of his logic, they did the only thing they could do—they began to ridicule his person. That is always the refuge of petty minds. When people cannot handle a logical argument they begin to attack the person, and try to destroy him. So they laughed at Jeremiah, poked fun at him, ridiculed him. Mockery is hard to bear, hard for the human spirit to take, and this was getting to Jeremiah.

Third, he discovered an unbearable tension within himself:

For whenever I speak, I cry out,
I shout, "Violence and destruction!"
For the word of the Lord has become for me
a reproach and derision all day long (Jer. 20:8).

Just a few chapters back, he had cried out in an ecstasy
of glory,

Thy words were found, and I ate them,
and thy words became to me a joy
and the delight of my heart . . . (Jer. 15:16).

Now he is saying "Lord, your word is a reproach and
derision to me. I wish I had never heard it!" And he
wants to quit preaching, but he cannot:

If I say, "I will not mention him,
or speak any more in his name,"
there is in my heart as it were a burning fire
shut up in my bones,
and I am weary with holding it in,
and I cannot (vs. 9).

How he is torn with this inner tension—fearful of pro-
claiming the truth, because it only subjects him to ridicule and scorn, and yet unable to quit. When he resolved
to keep still the fire of God burned in his bones and he
had to say something. Do you know anything of that?
Perhaps not with respect to public preaching—we are not
all called to that. But have you ever felt that you just had
to speak out? Some injustice, some moral perversity,
some scandalous conduct, some loveless hypocrisy was
occurring, and you just could not keep quiet about it.
And yet you knew that if you spoke out you would only
get into trouble, and nobody would thank you for it—
you would only upset the status quo and create strife—
but you could not contain yourself. Did you ever feel

that way? That was what Jeremiah was experiencing here—this tremendous struggle within himself against the proclamation of the word of God which only created more trouble.

The last thing he mentions is the sense he had of living in an atmosphere of total insecurity:

> For I hear many whispering.
>   Terror is on every side!
> "Denounce him! Let us denounce him!"
>   say all my familiar friends,
>   watching for my fall.
> "Perhaps he will be deceived,
>   then we can overcome him,
>   and take our revenge on him" (vs. 10).

There is not a person he can trust, not a one. Even his familiar friends, those he ate with, visited with, talked with, even they are whispering against him. There is terror on every side. Even the walls are bugged! There is no one he can trust. Even God has deceived him. That is a vivid description of the way our fears can seize our mind and distort reality to such a degree that we believe God himself is faithless to us. That is an accurate description, also, of a satanic attack, which is exactly what this is. When we begin to look at our circumstances, something within us begins to make everything look utterly black and dark.

If you have ever been in this predicament you know that it is nonsense to try to convince yourself intellectually that things are not bleak. It seems to be madness to deny what appears to be the reality of the situation. It looks exactly that way, and everybody tells you that is the way it is. But this is a lie. It is a distorted fantasy, not real at all. What the natural mind does to us when we try to see life on our own is to twist things all out of shape, conjuring up all kinds of lurid and gruesome spectacles which appear to be actual realities.

Counterattack

So faith comes to Jeremiah's rescue and begins to strengthen him. Faith counterattacks to uphold the tottering prophet. In verses 11 and 12, he says,

> But the Lord is with me as a dread warrior;
>   therefore my persecutors will stumble,
>   they will not overcome me.
> They will be greatly shamed,
>   for they will not succeed.
> Their eternal dishonor
>   will never be forgotten.
> O Lord of hosts, who triest the righteous,
>   who seest the heart and the mind,
> let me see thy vengeance upon them,
>   for to thee have I committed my cause.

That is the right thing to say; Jeremiah is now fighting back against the assault of lies. He begins now to reckon on reality, to count as truth what God had made known to him. That is the way to handle any frightening situation. You can be almost sure that the way you see it is not the way it really is. This is what you have to remember. Your mind is being assaulted, your thoughts twisted and distorted by a naturalistic view of things. And the only answer is to begin with God, the unchangeable One, the One who sees things the way they really are. Start with him and with what he has told you, and work from that back to your situation, and you will see it in an entirely different light.

This is what the prophet does here. He starts with God. "The Lord is with me [that is the first thing to remember], and he is a dread warrior [he knows how to fight, how to repel assaults]; therefore my persecutors will stumble [their plans are not going to work out], they will not overcome me. [In fact,] they will be greatly ashamed, for they will not succeed." Faith reassures him that this is what will happen. And this is the correct view, because this *is* what happened. And so he cries out,

> Sing to the Lord;
>   praise the Lord!
> For he has delivered the life of the needy
>   from the hand of evildoers (vs. 13).

That sounds like the account of the incident in Acts 16 when Paul and Silas, thrown into the dungeon and thrust into stocks at Philippi, began at midnight to sing praises to God, because their faith was fastened onto God and his greatness, and not upon their circumstances. And this is what Jeremiah learned to do—to sing praises to the Lord.

It would be great if we could end the account here. But Jeremiah is a very human man, and so he does as we often do—he sinks back into even greater despair!

> Cursed be the day
>   on which I was born!
> The day when my mother bore me,
>   let it not be blessed!
> Cursed be the man
>   who brought the news to my father,
> "A son is born to you,"
>   making him very glad (Jer. 20:14–15).

It must be about three o'clock in the morning now. Up until midnight he had been doing fine, but the last hour or two have really become intolerable. He is scrunched over in this cruel position, his feet are hurting, his hands are hurting, his head hurts, his back is raw and bloody, and he cannot soothe it in any way. So the situation gets to be too much again, and he begins to curse the day he was born.

> Let that man be like the cities
>   which the Lord overthrew without pity;
> let him hear a cry in the morning
>   and an alarm at noon,
> because he did not kill me in the womb;
>   so my mother would have been my grave,
>   and her womb for ever great.
> Why did I come forth from the womb
>   to see toil and sorrow,
>   and spend my days in shame? (vss. 16–18).

Have you ever said that? "Why was I ever born? I wish I'd never been born!" Well, what can help Jeremiah now? He does not tell us any more of what went on through the long, long night. But if you turn back to verse 3 and read what happens the next morning, you will see a different man: "On the morrow, when Pashhur released Jeremiah from the stocks, Jeremiah said to him, 'The Lord does not call your name Pashhur, but Terror on every side.'" That was what he himself had experienced during the long night: "I hear many whispering. Terror is on every side!" The name Pashhur means a "cleaver" or "splitter," a "divider." That evidently was the kind of man Pashhur was, always dividing people up, creating factions. Jeremiah says, "God is no longer going to call you Pashhur, but Terror on every side," that is, undependable, a frightening kind of man whom nobody dare trust. "Your leadership will be ignored, for no one can trust you."

> "For thus says the Lord: Behold, I will make you a terror to yourself and to all your friends. They shall fall by the sword of their enemies while you look on. And I will give all Judah into the hand of the king of Babylon; he shall carry them captive to Babylon, and shall slay them with the sword. Moreover, I will give all the wealth of the city, all its gains, all its prized belongings, and all the treasures of the kings of Judah into the hand of their enemies, who shall plunder them, and seize them, and carry them to Babylon. And you, Pashhur, and all who dwell in your house, shall go into captivity; to Babylon you shall go; and there you shall die, and there you shall be buried, you and all your friends, to whom you have prophesied falsely" (Jer. 20: 4–6).

Triumph over Trembling

Now he is as steady as a rock. What happened? Well, we do not know; we can only surmise. But I suggest that sometime through that long dark night, the burning in the bones of the prophet—the word of God—triumphed over the tremblings of his heart. The Word began to prove itself true. Jeremiah discovered what many of us have discovered in the hour of pressure, what the Word of God tells us—"Greater is he that is in you, than he that is in the world." Jeremiah began to think back upon the Word, its power, what it had accomplished in the past. And somewhere faith came to take hold of this struggling, weak, toppling man and strengthen him, so that when Pashhur came in the morning he was ready to meet him, look him straight in the eye, and tell him the message God had for him.

I thought of a verse in Paul's second letter to Timothy which seems to gather this up for us beautifully. Paul, in an hour of great turbulence in the world of his day, said, "Timothy, if we are faithless, he [Christ] remains faithful—for he cannot deny himself" (2 Tim. 2:13). Perhaps Jeremiah remembered what God had said in chapter 1: "Jeremiah, I am watching over my word to perform it." So even though it may take a while, even though things do not go right at first, do not be short-sighted and blame God, for he will "watch over his word to perform it."

8

Why the Land Mourns

Nebuchadnezzar made several expeditions against Jerusalem before it was finally overthrown and demolished, and its people led into captivity. But in this first invasion, during the reign of king Jehoiakim, Nebuchadnezzar took away into Babylon certain treasures from the temple at Jerusalem, and also certain young princes of Judah. Among them was a young man named Daniel, whose name you will recognize, and three of his friends: Hananiah, Azariah, and Mishael, who perhaps are better known to you by their Babylonian names—Shadrach, Meshach, and Abednego.

Jehoiakim was left in Jerusalem to be a vassal king, and he reigned seven more years. Then he rebelled against the government of Nebuchadnezzar, was deposed by another Babylonian invasion, and his son, Jehoiachin, also called Jeconiah, was put on the throne. He reigned for only three months, and then was taken as a captive to Babylon. His uncle, Zedekiah, one of the remaining sons of king Josiah, was put on the throne by Nebuchadnezzar to serve as a kind of caretaker king.

Rubbing the Lamp of Prayer

That brings us to the twenty-first chapter of Jeremiah with Zedekiah, weakest of all the kings of Judah and the last of the line, now on the throne. Nebuchadnezzar is sending up another army against Jerusalem, the city is under siege, and king Zedekiah now sends a hasty word to Jeremiah the prophet, asking him to intercede with God on their behalf:

> This is the word which came to Jeremiah from the Lord, when King Zedekiah sent to him Pashhur the son of Malchiah and Zephaniah the priest, the son of Ma-aseiah, saying, "Inquire of the Lord for us, for Nebuchadrezzar king of Babylon [this is merely another spelling of Nebuchadnezzar; both are used in Scripture] is making war against us; perhaps the Lord will deal with us according to all his wonderful deeds, and will make him withdraw from us" (Jer. 21:1-2).

That sounds very pious, does it not? King Zedekiah is asking the prophet to intercede with God, so that "maybe God will be his old, sweet, kindly self and let us go." There are many people who pray like this, who think that God is only for getting them out of trouble. They imagine that they can go on doing as they please, living the way they want, and ignoring all the efforts of God to check their course and correct their folly. Then, when they really get into trouble, all they have to do is pray, and God will come and set them free. A lot of people treat God that way, as this king was doing—expecting God to come through.

Of course, in that view, God is only a kind of heavenly genie, ready when you rub the lamp of prayer to appear

and say, "Yes, master; what do you want me to do?" But
God is not like that. God is sovereign. God moves according to his own purposes, and he does not play games
with us. He will not be mollified and placated by a temporary return to him when we get into difficulty, as
Zedekiah found out when he received God's answer to his
plea:

> Then Jeremiah said to them: "Thus you shall
> say to Zedekiah, 'Thus says the Lord, the God of
> Israel: Behold, I will turn back the weapons of war
> which are in your hands and with which you are
> fighting against the king of Babylon and against
> the Chaldeans who are besieging you outside the
> walls; and I will bring them together into the midst
> of this city. [Zedekiah, not only am I not going to
> help you; I'll hinder you. I will cause the weapons
> with which you are fighting to be turned against
> you.] I myself will fight against you with out-
> stretched hand and strong arm, in anger, and in
> fury, and in great wrath. And I will smite the in-
> habitants of this city, both man and beast; they
> shall die of a great pestilence. Afterward, says the
> Lord, I will give Zedekiah king of Judah, and his
> servants, and the people in this city who survive
> the pestilence, sword, and famine, into the hand of
> Nebuchadrezzar king of Babylon and into the hand
> of their enemies, into the hand of those who seek
> their lives. He shall smite them with the edge of
> the sword; he shall not pity them, or spare them,
> or have compassion'" (Jer. 21:3–7).

There is a way this king could have found the mercy
and grace of God, of course. Had he knelt before God
and confessed his evil deeds, calling upon God out of a
heart of contrition and repentance, God would have turned

and met him. He promises that it is still not too late wherever there is a real change of heart. But God is not there simply for bargaining, someone to whom we can call for help only out of a fervid desire to escape the consequences of our folly. Verse 10 summarizes the thrust of this chapter: " 'For I have set my face against this city for evil and not for good, says the Lord: it shall be given into the hand of the king of Babylon, and he shall burn it with fire.' " That should have been enough to upset this king and turn him around, but it was not. So in chapter 22 God says to the prophet, "I want you to go up and talk to the king himself, face to face." This is the first time Jeremiah is sent to deliver a message directly to the king himself:

> Thus says the Lord: "Go down to the house of the king of Judah, and speak there this word, and say, 'Hear the word of the Lord, O King of Judah, who sit on the throne of David, you, and your servants, and your people who enter these gates' " (Jer. 22:1–2).

So Jeremiah goes down to the palace, and comes before the king himself. From this point through the end of chapter 25 is a record of the message Jeremiah gave before this king. In this great message Jeremiah traces before the king what has gone wrong in his nation. As we face somewhat similar troubles in our own day, Jeremiah's message can help us draw some very important conclusions related to these deeply confused times.

These ancient prophets, by the way, were not like court priests or preachers. Jeremiah's appearance at the palace was not like having Billy Graham hold meetings for the president in the White House, nor even like having John

Knox thunder away before Mary Queen of Scots, expounding the Scriptures. Rather, these prophets were sent to the kings with direct messages, right from the mind of God.

The Tasks of Government

The heart of Jeremiah's message was that two areas of the national life were terribly wrong. Jeremiah sets these before the king in great power. The first area is summarized for us in the opening verses of chapter 23:

> "Woe to the shepherds who destroy and scatter the sheep of my pasture!" says the Lord. Therefore thus says the Lord, the God of Israel, concerning the shepherds who care for my people: "You have scattered my flock, and have driven them away, and you have not attended to them. Behold, I will attend to you for your evil doings," says the Lord (Jer. 23:1–2).

Who are these shepherds? They are the kings of the nation. Rulers and government leaders are the shepherds of God. All through the Old and the New Testaments this idea is behind God's concept of government. Governmental leaders are to be shepherds of the people, watching over them and taking care of them. As we listen to the message developed here by the prophet, we will find in it a recognition of the proper tasks of government. What are governors and presidents and leaders for? In one great verse the prophet sets forth the answer:

> Thus says the Lord: Do justice and righteousness, and deliver from the hand of the oppressor him who has been robbed. And do no wrong or violence to the alien, the fatherless, and the widow, nor shed innocent blood in this place (Jer. 22:3).

This king, and others like him, had failed to do these things. Notice that they were first to set an example of justice and righteousness themselves. Rulers, leaders, and elected officials are to be an example of righteousness and justice before the people. This is why it is so serious when politicians and elected officials do things which are wrong. Since Watergate, people have been saying, "Why make such a fuss over a little corruption in business or industry—look at the politicians in Washington! Everybody does this sort of thing, so what's the big deal?"

The answer is that every governmental leader, every politician elected or appointed to an official position in government, from the president on down in our own country, is, as Paul makes clear to us in Romans 13, a minister of God. He may not be a believer, but he himself is a minister, an agent of God, and is to represent God's standard of righteousness and judgment. Therefore, when these elected officials or leaders of the land—kings or presidents or whatever they may be—are guilty of wrongdoing, the effect of their wrongdoing is greatly intensified, is far greater than if they were just ordinary citizens. This is why the Watergate affair was such a serious matter. And Jeremiah was sent to tell this king that he had failed to correct the wrongs of the land, had failed to "deliver from the hand of the oppressor him who had been robbed," and had failed himself to be a pattern of justice and righteousness.

Then the second responsibility of government leaders is: "Do no wrong or violence to the alien, the fatherless, and the widow." These are the minority groups in any country, the weak, the helpless. You will notice that the king is told here that it is his task to see that *he* does no violence to them. Here is a recognition of the power of government to hurt the weak, a recognition that government finds it *easy* to do so in its management of events. Bureaucracy can make it easy to turn a deaf ear and to be unavailable to those who are really in trouble. Special care must be taken by any government to watch over the weak within the nation—the aliens, the foreigners, those with different cultural patterns; and the widows and orphans—those with no one to plead their cause. This is the task of government.

And the third responsibility of government leaders is to keep the courts honest and just: "Do not shed innocent blood in this place." The task of government is to see that justice is available in a courtroom, that the guilty are found out and the innocent are freed, and that innocent people are not punished wrongly by the court. This king had failed in this, and the prophet spells out the details of his failure:

> "Woe to him who builds his house by unrighteousness,
>   and his upper rooms by injustice;
> who makes his neighbor serve him for nothing,
>   and does not give him his wages;
> who says, 'I will build myself a great house
>   with spacious upper rooms,'
> and cuts out windows for it,
>   paneling it with cedar,
>   and painting it with vermilion" (Jer. 22:13–14).

Even in those days they had trouble with rulers embellishing their own private homes! And the amazing thing is that when this nation of Judah was bankrupt and in deep trouble, its treasures being looted from the temple and the city itself surrounded by an army, the king utilized his power and caused his subjects to build a house for him. Jeremiah says, "Do you think you are a king because you compete in cedar?" "Just because you can build a bigger house than someone else, does that make you a king?" Then he refers him to the standard of his father, Josiah:

> "Did not your father eat and drink
> and do justice and righteousness?
> Then it was well with him.
> He judged the cause of the poor and needy;
> then it was well.
> [Then he asks this insightful question.]
> Is not this to know me?
>   says the Lord" (vss. 15–16).

That is what it means to know God—to let your actions be changed by the knowledge you have of God who watches over the needy and the weak.

Three Bad Kings

The prophet gives three bad examples of kings in Judah. In verses 11 and 12 he refers to Shallum, which is another name of Jehoahaz, who went down to Egypt: "He shall return here no more, but in the place where they have carried him captive, there shall he die, and he shall never see this land again." Another example is Jehoiakim, one of the sons of Josiah:

> Therefore thus says the Lord concerning
> Jehoiakim the son of Josiah, king of Judah:
> "They shall not lament for him, saying,
> 'Ah my brother!' or 'Ah sister!'
> They shall not lament for him, saying,
> 'Ah lord!' or 'Ah his majesty!'
> [Nobody is going to feel sorry when he is gone.]
> With the burial of an ass he shall be buried,
> dragged and cast forth beyond the gates of
> Jerusalem" (vss. 18–19).

Then still a third is Coniah, another name for Jehoiachin, son of Jehoiakim:

> "As I live, says the Lord, though Coniah the son of Jehoiakim, king of Judah, were the signet ring on my right hand, yet I would tear you off and give you into the hand of those who seek your life, into the hand of those of whom you are afraid, even into the hand of Nebuchadrezzar king of Babylon and into the hand of the Chaldeans" (vss. 24–25).

This man Coniah, just 23 years old, and after a reign of only three months, was deposed and carried to Babylon, and spent the rest of a long life in captivity. God says an amazing thing about him in verse 30:

> Thus says the Lord:
> "Write this man down as childless,
>   a man who shall not succeed in his days;
> for none of his offspring shall succeed
>   in sitting on the throne of David,
>   and ruling again in Judah."

This is a very significant verse, for it means the end of the Solomonic line of succession. Up to this time, all the kings of Judah had been descendants of King Solomon, son of David. But with this man, that line of succession ended. No more was a man of that line allowed to rule on the throne of Judah. This affects the story of Jesus in the New Testament, for when you trace the genealogy of Joseph, the stepfather of Jesus, you discover that Joseph was the son of David through this man Coniah, or Jehoiachin, and thus had lost the right to sit on the throne of Judah. Had Jesus been his natural son, he would never have had the right to be king of Judah. But because he was the son of Mary, who was likewise a descendant of David through Nathan, a brother of Solomon, Jesus therefore had the right to the throne of David. It is amazing how God ties history together and works in marvelous ways we cannot anticipate!

Jeremiah is now given a vision of the true shepherd. For the first time in this great prophecy he does as Isaiah frequently did—he lifts up his eyes, looks down through the centuries, and sees the coming of One who would fulfill God's ideal, and on beyond that to the time when he will return again to actually carry out God's requirement for justice:

> "Behold the days are coming, says the Lord, when I will raise up for David a righteous Branch, and he shall reign as king and deal wisely, and shall execute justice and righteousness in the land. In his days Judah will be saved, and Israel will dwell securely. [Lest we wonder who this would be, he tells us how to identify him.] And this is the name by which he will be called: 'The Lord is our righteousness' " (Jer. 23:5–6).

That is the name applied to Jesus by the apostle Paul in 1 Corinthians 1:30: ". . . Christ Jesus, whom God made our wisdom, our righteousness and sanctification and redemption." He himself is our righteousness. So the prophet sees him coming as God's rightful king, and one day to come again so that "Judah will be saved, and Israel will dwell securely."

Ungodliness Has Gone Forth

Corruption in government was the first area of national life which was wrong. But the prophet is led now to speak of something still worse:

Concerning the prophets:
My heart is broken within me,
    all my bones shake;
I am like a drunken man,
    like a man overcome by wine,
because of the Lord
    and because of his holy words.
For the land is full of adulterers;
    because of the curse the land mourns,
    and the pastures of the wilderness are
        dried up (Jer. 23:9–10).

What is wrong? Well, back of the king was the prophet. It is bad enough when the king goes wrong, but when the preachers who are there to correct the king go wrong, there is no hope for that land. And here were the prophets, who should have set the king right, prophesying and preaching the wrong things. So there was a fatal cancer at the heart of this nation which could not be cured. That is why judgment had to come. God says in verse 15:

Therefore thus says the Lord of hosts concerning the prophets:
    "Behold, I will feed them with wormwood,
        and give them poisoned water to drink;
    for from the prophets of Jerusalem
        ungodliness has gone forth into all the land."

We wonder what has happened in America. We wonder where our national strength has gone, why we seem to grow weaker and weaker instead of stronger and stronger, why, when we have the greatest military might the world has ever known, we exercise less and less influence among the nations of earth. But behind the government, you see, is the church. Every land, eventually, is governed by what is going on in the church, by what is going on among the people of God. That is why Jesus said, "You are the salt of the earth, you are the light of the world."

Jeremiah points out some of the things that were wrong among these preachers, these prophets. First, verse 16: "Thus says the Lord of hosts: 'Do not listen to the words of the prophets who prophesy to you, filling you with vain hopes . . .'" They were filling the people with vain hopes, telling them that things were going to be all right. They preached messages to convince them that man would work out his difficulties and everything would be fine—they could count on it. But they were vain hopes. Why? Well, secondly, he reveals, "'. . . they speak visions of their own minds, not from the mouth of the Lord.'" That is why they are vain hopes. They are just the prophets' own ideas of what is happening in the nation, their own subjective viewpoints of what is wrong in life, their own opinions and religious ideas. And that is all they are worth. They have not sat and listened to the voice of God. Verse 18 says,

For who among them has stood in the council of the Lord
  to perceive and to hear his word,
  or who has given heed to his word and listened?

That is what was wrong with the prophets—they were preaching themselves, not God. And that is what has happened in America. Turn back the record forty or fifty years in this nation, to the time of the theological movement known as "German Rationalism," when preachers began to turn from the Scriptures and to preach their own messages. The amazing thing is that this movement has influenced not only what we call "liberal" churches, but many evangelicals, as well.

At seminars for pastors which we hold regularly at our

church, we study the Word of God together with men from all over the nation and learn what God is saying today to the people of this land about the resources and the tremendous basis of operation that God has made available to us. At the close of the seminars the pastors, are asked to give their evaluation of what has happened to them. It is always interesting to me to see how many of these men express anger at the fact that in their previous training they had learned little or nothing of how to teach the Scriptures. They shake their heads and say, "Why didn't we learn this in school? Why weren't we taught this?" They are literally angry, because as they look back on their own ministries they find that they have been giving out their own ideas, having never been taught to expound the Word of God, to stand in the council of God and to hear his Word. That is what wrecks a nation, because then there is no correction of the evils of government.

What happens next is that they give false assurances:

> "They say continually to those who despise the word of the Lord, 'It shall be well with you'; and to every one who stubbornly follows his own heart, they say, 'No evil shall come upon you'" (Jer. 23:17).

That is what we are hearing today, is it not? The "new morality" tells us, "Don't worry, young people. If you love each other you can do anything you want and nothing will happen. No evil will befall you." Prophets of today are saying to our generation, "You can run off with your neighbor's wife, you can cheat on your income tax, you can do all these things and you don't have to worry about it. No evil is going to fall, no harmful results will come."

And that is why a nation begins to fall apart and lose its strength.

The last charge against the prophets is that they claimed the very authority of God:

> "Behold, I am against the prophets, says the Lord, who use their tongues and say, 'Says the Lord.' Behold, I am against those who prophesy lying dreams, says the Lord, and who tell them and lead my people astray by their lies and their recklessness, when I did not send them or charge them; so they do not profit this people at all, says the Lord" (vss. 31–32).

They claimed God's authority to say things that God did not tell them to say at all. And that is what hurts a nation. When prophets or preachers tell lies in the name of the Lord, the heart of the nation is eaten away and the people fall apart morally because there is no faithful word from God.

The Right Way

Now the prophet draws the contrasts of the true ministry. The first thing a preacher should do is to stand before God:

"I did not send the prophets,
  yet they ran;
I did not speak to them,
  yet they prophesied.
But if they had stood in my council,
  then they would have proclaimed my words to my people,
and they would have turned them from their evil way,
  and from the evil of their doings" (Jer. 23:21–22).

A man has to stand before God and hear God speak to *him*, first. That is the first thing. Years ago, when I was a young pastor, I found I was preaching messages I had more or less borrowed from great Bible teachers—not taking them verbatim, but leaning heavily upon the ministry of men whom I admired. Every young man does that as he starts out in the ministry. But gradually I learned that God had to say something to my heart first, that I could not borrow somebody else's fire. It had to be fire in my own soul, something God was saying to me, or it could never set fire in the hearts of other people. This is what God says is paramount—we must stand in his council and hear his words.

Then what? Verse 28: "Let the prophet who has a dream tell the dream, but let him who has my word speak my word faithfully." That is the business of a preacher—to take what God has said and set it before the people without diluting it, to say faithfully what God has said, for that is what will save a nation from hurt and preserve it from harm. God goes on to show what can be accomplished through such a ministry: "Is not my word like fire, says the Lord, and like a hammer which breaks the rock in pieces?" (vs. 29) God's Word pounds away with honesty and realism, setting before people exactly what is happening, exactly where they are. His desire is for them to see his loving heart, urging them as a nation to turn around from what is tearing them apart.

In the last section of this great message, which you can read in chapters 24 and 25, Jeremiah refers back to a message he had given earlier to another king, in which he showed how a king ought to react when God is judging a people or a nation. How do you react when you are under the chastisement of God, when God has found that the only way he can get through to you is to bring trouble into your life, to catch you up short? What are you to do? The prophet sets before the king three things that he is to remember.

God's Best for You

The first, in chapter 24, is to accept the judging hand of God as the very best hope for you. In this chapter the prophet was shown a vision of two big baskets of figs. One was a basket of good figs, the other of rotten, stinking figs. God said, "These figs are like the people. The good figs are those who are to be carried captive to Babylon." That is astonishing, because if you had lived in Judah in those days, you would have said, "The worst thing that could happen to me would be to be taken captive by Nebuchadnezzar and carried away from this land into Babylon." But God would have said to you, "You are absolutely wrong! That is the best thing that could happen to you." In fact, he says,

> "I will set my eyes upon them for good, and I will bring them back to this land. I will build them up, and not tear them down; I will plant them, and not uproot them. I will give them a heart to know that I am the Lord; and they shall be my people and I will be their God, for they shall return to me with their whole heart" (Jer. 24:6-7).

"This is what will cure them," he says. "This will set them straight." So that what looked like the worst thing to them was actually the best thing in God's eyes. "But if you stay in this land," he says, "if you are not carried away captive, that will be the worst thing that could happen to you." For he says,

> "I will make them a horror to all the kingdoms of the earth, to be a reproach, a byword, a taunt, and a curse in all the places where I shall drive them. And I will send sword, famine, and pestilence upon them, until they shall be utterly destroyed from the land which I gave to them and their fathers" (vss. 9–10).

God's admonition is to accept what he is doing with you as the best thing for you, and to know that his love will triumph.

The second thing he sets before the king, the second principle we are to learn from this, is that we are to wait for the measured end that God has in view. The prophet says to this king,

> "This whole land shall become a ruin and a waste, and these nations shall serve the king of Babylon seventy years. Then after seventy years are completed, I will punish the king of Babylon and that nation, and the land of the Chaldeans, for their iniquity, says the Lord, making the land an everlasting waste" (Jer. 25:11–12).

That was a specified period of time: seventy years. As we know from other Scriptures, this was the length of time that Israel had failed to allow the land to enjoy its sabbath. For four hundred and ninety years they had lived in this land, and not once did they ever observe the sabbatical year, to let the land lie fallow for one year. So seventy of those sabbatical years had stacked up, and God said, "I will send you to Babylon for seventy years, while the land enjoys its sabbath." God always has a time limit on what he does with us. Remember the fellow who said, "My favorite Scripture is where it says, 'And it came to pass . . .' It is such a comfort to know that it didn't come to stay; it came to pass!" It will pass. And so, under the hand of God's judgment, wait out his measured time, knowing that it shall come to *pass*.

The third and last principle the chapter gives us is that God says the prophet is to expect a widening circle of cleansing, beginning with Judah, but reaching out to all the nations around. And in two vivid figures he describes how God works. It is like a cup which you drink from, then pass it to your neighbor and he drinks from it, who in turn gives it to another neighbor. And so the cup is sent around all the nations, first making them drunk with the judgment of God, but also bringing them into repentance before God. The king is told, "For behold, I begin to work evil at the city which is called by my name, and shall you go unpunished?" (vs. 29) And as God begins to work in your life, you know that others are also going to be subjected to the same judgment as you, and they will learn from you. God's cleansing hand will reach out.

God's work is finally described as a mighty storm:

"Thus says the Lord of hosts:
Behold, evil is going forth
    from nation to nation,
and a great tempest is stirring
    from the farthest parts of the earth!" (Jer. 25:32)

The process will keep on building up into a great and mighty storm which will bring at last the final judgment of God. It may be that we' are in those days, and God is judging his people today. "The time is come that judgment must begin at the house of God," says Peter. And as we are subjected to it—our hearts searched and our minds open before God—and we are brought to repentance and to confession and to turning from our evil in the church of God, that judgment is going to reach out to the nation around, and to nations beyond. And God's great judgment storm will come to pass when at last all the fearsome scenes of Revelation are brought before us, in order that the world may be cleansed. Then God can begin the new heavens and the new earth which are promised to us. That is what God is doing. We are part of a great, mighty, sweeping movement of God in the history of this day, and we ought to bow before him and give grateful thanks that we are in his hands, the God of mercy.

9

Who Knows?

When the family of Alexander Solzhenitsyn was able to join him in Switzerland, escaping the tyranny and persecution of the Soviets, the Free World rejoiced. Solzhenitsyn has become a hero of our day, admired for his stand alone against the power of a godless state, and for the way he has exposed so courageously its hideous evil. It has been noteworthy to see how he has been hated and persecuted, and yet protected, for God's hand has been upon him and has kept him safe in the midst of grave and terrible dangers. He is in many ways a modern picture of what Jeremiah was back in the days of Judah—a brave prophet, standing almost alone before a godless government, enduring continual threat to his life, yet courageously speaking the message God had for him to give.

Verse 1 of chapter 26 tells us that it was in the beginning of the reign of Jehoiakim the son of Josiah, king of Judah, that this word came from the Lord. Jeremiah is looking back to the days when Jehoiakim first came to the throne. An incident occurred then which he had not recorded for us earlier, but which he now brings before

us. God had sent him to this godless, weak, and vain king
with another message of warning about the coming destruction that would await a nation which did not repent.
Yet hidden in it is that heartbeat of God which longs to
have a people delivered, to find for them a way of repentance; you see this in verse 3: "It may be they will
listen, and every one turn from his evil way, that I may
repent of the evil which I intend to do to them because
of their evil doings." As we see repeatedly throughout
Scripture, God does not delight in judgment. He longs
that his hand may be lifted, that a people will turn and
listen, will repent, so that he may sigh with relief, and
not have to come through with the harshness of judgment.
But then he goes on in verses 4 through 6:

> "You shall say to them, 'Thus says the Lord: If
> you will not listen to me, to walk in my law which I
> have set before you, and to heed the words of my
> servants the prophets whom I send to you urgently,
> though you have not heeded, then I will make
> this house like Shiloh [a city north of Jerusalem
> which by this time was barren and desolate], and
> I will make this city a curse for all the nations of
> the earth.' "

These are not empty threats. God means what he says.
He is sovereign in the affairs of men. He governs the
relations of nations. One of the encouraging messages of
this book to our day is to remind us again that God is in
control of the nations. They will do what he tells them
to do, they will go where he sends them to go, whether
they like it or not. Nations are not independent, sovereign
states, as we often term them. They are sovereign as far
as men's affairs are concerned, but not before God. God

is sovereign. His threats will be carried out exactly as he said.

Indicted for Treason

In the verses which follow, you have what we might call "the impeachment of Jeremiah":

> The priests and the prophets and all the people heard Jeremiah speaking these words in the house of the Lord. And when Jeremiah had finished speaking all that the Lord had commanded him to speak to all the people, then the priests and the prophets and all the people laid hold of him, saying, "You shall die! Why have you prophesied in the name of the Lord, saying, 'This house shall be like Shiloh, and this city shall be desolate, without inhabitant'?" And all the people gathered about Jeremiah in the house of the Lord (Jer. 26:7-9).

This is an official gathering, a trial, at which Jeremiah has been impeached by the people. And the religious authorities of the nation, the priests and the prophets, are behind this. They have laid a serious charge, a charge of treason, against the prophet. These people felt that because the temple was God's house, God would defend that temple no matter what happened within it. They had an idea which many have today—that if something belongs to God, or he has said it is his, he will never let anything bad happen to it. They thought the temple was inviolate, and that the city was protected, because it was the city of God. They could look back over hundreds of years of history when God had indeed protected this city. Here was a people who were saying, "It can't happen here!" But Jeremiah said it would happen, and was therefore charged with blasphemy and treason against the temple of God and the city of God.

The rest of chapter 26, beginning at verse 10, gives the account of his trial. It was to be held before the princes of Judah: "When the princes of Judah heard these things, they came up from the king's house to the house of the Lord and took their seat in the entry of the New Gate of the house of the Lord." This was the judgment chamber where the trial was to be held. Among these princes undoubtedly were Daniel and his three friends, Mishael, Hananiah, and Azariah, for these were all nobles of the house of Judah, and this episode occurred before they were led captive into Babylon. So there were some godly men among these princes.

> Then the priests and the prophets said to the princes and to all the people, "This man deserves the sentence of death, because he has prophesied against this city, as you have heard with your own ears" (vs. 11).

This is, therefore, a very serious charge; Jeremiah is on trial for his life. In verses 12 through 15 we have Jeremiah's defense, and it is a very interesting one:

> Then Jeremiah spoke to all the princes and all the people, saying, "The Lord sent me to prophesy against this house and this city all the words you have heard. Now therefore amend your ways and your doings, and obey the voice of the Lord your God, and the Lord will repent of the evil which he has pronounced against you."

Notice that there is not the slightest deviation on his part. This would have been the time, if he were so inclined, to have said to these people, "Now just a minute.

I want to make one thing perfectly clear! I have indeed prophesied, but I didn't mean to have it taken as seriously as you are doing. I'm sure that if you'll let me off, I can intercede before God on your behalf, and perhaps he'll change his mind." But he does not say that. He does not alter his word one bit: "Amend your ways and your doings, and the Lord will repent of the evil which he has pronounced against you." This took courage! Then he speaks about himself:

> "But as for me, behold, I am in your hands. Do with me as seems good and right to you. Only know for certain that if you put me to death, you will bring innocent blood upon yourselves and upon this city and its inhabitants, for in truth the Lord sent me to you to speak all these words in your ears" (vss. 14–15).

Jeremiah does what the people of God have been exhorted to do all through the Scriptures at times like this: leave it in God's hands. If you are charged unjustly with something of which you are not guilty, do not try to defend yourself. The battle is God's. He will work it out. Put yourself in the hands of God, and he will see you through. This is what Peter says about the Lord Jesus: "When he was reviled, he did not revile in return; when he suffered, he did not threaten; but he trusted to him who judges justly" (1 Pet. 2:23). This is what Jeremiah does. So often we are so concerned lest somebody think something wrong about us. It is perfectly all right to explain things as far as possible. But when it is evident that nobody is willing to listen, then just put it in God's hands. He knows what he is doing.

And what was the outcome of this trial? "Then the princes and all the people said to the priests and the prophets. 'This man does not deserve the sentence of death, for he has spoken to us in the name of the Lord our God' " (vs. 16). The official verdict of this trial was acquittal for Jeremiah. God moved in the hearts of these princes, and I am sure that if Daniel and others like him were among them, they were taking the leadership to see that God's will was done.

Then certain of the elders stood up, in the way that Jews had, to confirm the sentence of the court by the actions of God in history. They reminded the court of two incidents—one in the past, and one very recent—which confirmed the action that was taken. One concerned Micah the prophet, whose book we have in our Scriptures. Micah had stood before king Hezekiah and had said words similar to those of Jeremiah, predicting judgment against Jerusalem and the land. Hezekiah had repented, and God spared that land, in line with his promise. So this confirmed the action they were taking with Jeremiah.

The more recent incident concerned a prophet named Uriah, a man about whom we know nothing else, who had stood before king Jehoiakim himself and had said similar words. (This indicates that Jeremiah was not alone in the land in those days; there were other voices. Habakkuk was also ministering in the land at this time.) The king was very angry and ordered Uriah to be put to death. Uriah fled to Egypt, but the king pursued him, brought him back to Judah, and slew him. King Jehoiakim had refused to repent and great evil was brought upon the land as a result. Now the word of the elders is, "We are about to bring great evil upon ourselves." Thus they confirmed the verdict of the court.

The last verse tells us the outcome: "But the hand of Ahikam the son of Shaphan was with Jeremiah so that he was not given over to the people to be put to death (vs. 24).

Thongs and Yoke-Bars

In the next chapter we leap over a period of about twelve years to the time of Zedekiah, the last king of Judah. Nebuchadnezzar has already come up against Jerusalem and has made Zedekiah a vassal-king, serving under his authority and power. But now a council of the nations surrounding Israel has sent ambassadors to Jerusalem to plot a rebellion against Nebuchadnezzar. On this occasion God has a word for Jeremiah to give to the king, and it is accompanied by another visual aid to heighten the impact of the message:

> In the beginning of the reign of Zedekiah the son of Josiah, king of Judah, this word came to Jeremiah from the Lord. Thus the Lord said to me: "Make yourself thongs and yoke-bars, and put them on your neck" (Jer. 27:1–2).

This time Jeremiah had to go down to the carpenter shop and have made for himself a large wooden yoke of the kind they used to have in the days of the Old West to yoke a team of oxen together. He wore this around his neck, evidently for months at a time. He also had others made which were sent back by the ambassador to these surrounding countries—Tyre, Sidon, Edom, Moab, and all the other countries around Judah—so that they might wear them. For God was seeking to impress upon them a tremendous fact which he declared in a message accompanying these yokes:

> "It is I who by great power and my outstretched arm have made the earth, with the men and ani-

mals that are on the earth, and I give it to whom-
ever it seems right to me. Now I have given all
these lands into the hand of Nebuchadnezzar, the
king of Babylon, my servant, and I have given him
also the beasts of the field to serve him. All the
nations shall serve him and his son and his grand-
son, until the time of his own land comes [God
has a time of judgment for the nations he uses to
judge, as well]; then many nations and great kings
shall make him their slave.

" ' "But if any nation or kingdom will not serve
this Nebuchadnezzar king of Babylon, and put its
neck under the yoke of the king of Babylon, I will
punish that nation with the sword, with famine,
and with pestilence, says the Lord, until I have
consumed it by his hand" (Jer. 27:5–8).

Daniel, who was a captive in Babylon during this time,
tells us of a dream that occurred to Nebuchadnezzar. In
the dream, the king saw a great image which depicted
him as the head of all the nations of that day, just as God
declares in this message.

This is one of the things which has puzzled many people throughout history. Why does God raise up a godless
people, a cruel and sometimes vicious people, calling them
his servants, and giving them authority and power which
nobody can contravene? Why does he let them move out
in depredation and violence against other people, sometimes godly people who are turning from their godliness
and need to be caught up short? Why does God do this?
History records that it happens again and again, and
God is doing it once more in our own day. This is why
we have seen the sudden, remarkable rise of godless com-
munism; it is God's hand, to judge his own people. The
Communists are allowed to rule and to do certain things

with impunity, but God insists that his judgments be carried out this way. One of the great lessons we can learn from this book is that God is in control.

Nebuchadnezzar's supremacy is the beginning of what Daniel calls "the times of the Gentiles." Remember that Jesus said that the times of the Gentiles would not end until Jerusalem would be taken again by the Jews: "Jerusalem will be trodden down by the Gentiles, until the times of the Gentiles are fulfilled." In June of 1967, Jerusalem, the old city, was recaptured by the Jews. For the first time in all the centuries since Nebuchadnezzar's day, the old city was back in the hands of the Jews, under the sovereign authority of the Jews. This marks, I believe, the last of the times of the Gentiles, the last of those strange periods of history God has marked out in which his people would be subjected to slavery under the nations around them, until God's purposes are fulfilled. This message is followed now by the prophet's personal admonition to these kings:

> So do not listen to your prophets, your diviners, your dreamers, your soothsayers, or your sorcerers, who are saying to you, 'You shall not serve the king of Babylon.' For it is a lie which they are prophesying to you, with the result that you will be removed far from your land, and I will drive you out, and you will perish" (vss. 9–10).

This is the key to this section. God is saying that in the days when a nation begins to disintegrate and lose its national coherence, false prophets will arise who will try to confuse people by conflicting words. It is not difficult to see that in our day this type of phenomenon is occurring again. And along with the false prophets, the occult will rise in popularity and influence, as indicated here:

". . . your diviners, your dreamers, your soothsayers, or
your sorcerers . . ." Their prophecies are nothing but
lying dreams, Jeremiah says. He reaffirms this to Zedekiah
personally in verses 12 through 15, and then he reminds
the priests and all the people:

> "Thus says the Lord: Do not listen to the words of
> your prophets who are prophesying to you, saying,
> 'Behold, the vessels of the Lord's house will now
> shortly be brought back from Babylon,' for it is a
> lie which they are prophesying to you. Do not listen
> to them; serve the king of Babylon and live" (vss.
> 16–17).

Is that not amazing? Think of the courage it took for
this man to stand up and say, "Go out and surrender to
the king of Babylon. Serve him, and you'll survive." No
wonder they laid a charge of treason against him as recorded in chapter 32. And yet Jeremiah is uttering the
word of God concerning the nation, and faithfully warns
them of the fatal results of unbelief.

An Ungodly Optimist

In chapter 28 we have a very clear picture of the power
and effect of these false prophets. One of them, Hananiah,
is singled out for us. This false prophet directly chal-
lenges Jeremiah:

> In that same year, at the beginning of the reign
> of Zedekiah king of Judah, in the fifth month of
> the fourth year, Hananiah the son of Azur, the
> prophet from Gibeon, spoke to me in the house
> of the Lord, in the presence of the priests and all
> the people, saying, "Thus says the Lord of hosts,
> the God of Israel: I have broken the yoke of the
> king of Babylon. Within two years I will bring

back to this place all the vessels of the Lord's
house, which Nebuchadnezzar king of Babylon
took away from this place and carried to Babylon.
I will also bring back to this place Jeconiah the
son of Jehoiakim, king of Judah, and all the exiles
from Judah who went to Babylon, says the Lord,
for I will break the yoke of the king of Babylon"
(vss. 1–4).

That was an optimistic message, just what they all
wanted to hear. Notice how this prophet speaks: "Thus
says the Lord of hosts, the God of Israel . . ."—the same
formula Jeremiah himself uses. Can you imagine the confusion which must have spread among the people and
among the rulers and prophets and priests when they
heard both these prophets saying that they spoke by the
power of God, both claiming that it was the Lord who
had given them the message, and yet delivering two absolutely contradictory messages? Jeremiah was saying
they would be in Babylon for seventy years; Hananiah
now says they will be there for two. Which one is right?
Who knows? Notice how Jeremiah replies:

Then the prophet Jeremiah spoke to Hananiah
the prophet in the presence of the priests and all
the people who were standing in the house of the
Lord; and the prophet Jeremiah said, "Amen! May
the Lord do so; may the Lord make the words
which you have prophesied come true, and bring
back to this place from Babylon the vessels of the
house of the Lord, and all the exiles. ["There's
nothing I'd like better," says Jeremiah. "I wish it
were true, I wish you were right. But . . ."] Yet
hear now this word which I speak in your hearing
and in the hearing of all the people. The prophets
who preceded you and me from ancient times

prophesied war, famine, and pestilence against
many countries and great kingdoms. As for the
prophet who prophesies peace, when the word of
that prophet comes to pass, then it will be known
that the Lord has truly sent the prophet" (Jer.
28:5–9).

He does what all the prophets have done. The only way
you can ever tell that a man is from God, and does not
represent some other voice, is that his prophecies must
be one hundred percent true! He is allowed no margin for
error, no guesswork. If a prophet's predictions are ever
erroneous, that man is clearly not a prophet of God. That
is a very important precept to learn from this account.
Jeremiah says, "We'll wait and see! Two years are not
too long to wait. Let's just wait and see. You say it's going to happen in two years? All right; the man whose
prophecy comes true is the true prophet of God." But
notice the arrogance of this man Hananiah:

Then the prophet Hananiah took the yoke-bars
from the neck of Jeremiah the prophet, and broke
them. And Hananiah spoke in the presence of all
the people, saying, "Thus says the Lord: Even so
will I break the yoke of Nebuchadnezzar king of
Babylon from the neck of all the nations within
two years" (vss. 10–11).

Thus he emphasized the false message he had given by
this dramatic action. He took the wooden yoke from around
Jeremiah's neck and broke it in two, and said, "That's
what God is going to do to the yoke of Babylon." But
Jeremiah, the account says, "went his way." It was not
his problem, it was God's problem. It was up to God to
defend his prophet and his prophecy. And if God did not

do it—well, then *he* had lost the battle. So Jeremiah just waits patiently.

How does it work out?

> Sometime after the prophet Hananiah had broken the yoke-bars from off the neck of Jeremiah the prophet, the word of the Lord came to Jeremiah: "Go, tell Hananiah, 'Thus says the Lord: You have broken wooden bars, but I will make in their place bars of iron'" (Jer. 28:12–13).

"There is no escape. You cannot beat God. Do you think you can maneuver and manipulate things, and evade what God has said? There is no way. If you try it, things just get worse." Have you ever tried to manipulate God? Then you know what he means when he says, "I will make bars of iron if you break the wooden ones."

> " 'For thus says the Lord of hosts, the God of Israel: I have put upon the neck of all these nations an iron yoke of servitude to Nebuchadnezzar king of Babylon, and they shall serve him, for I have given to him even the beasts of the field.'" [When God does that, no man can contravene.] And Jeremiah the prophet said to the prophet Hananiah, "Listen, Hananiah, the Lord has not sent you, and you have made this people trust in a lie. [Now he is much more bold, for he had a direct word from God.] Therefore thus says the Lord: 'Behold, I will remove you from the face of the earth. This very year you shall die, because you have uttered rebellion against the Lord'" (vss. 14–16).

This was a phophecy you could check very quickly. "This very year you shall die!" Well, what happened? "In that same year, in the seventh month, the prophet Hananiah died" (vs. 17). God honored his prophet and sustained him in the midst of this test.

The Way Out Is to Stay Put

In chapter 29, of which we will read only certain sections, there is a letter which Jeremiah wrote to the exiles in Babylon. The confusion was as great in Babylon as it was in Judah. These four thousand or more captives who had gone to Babylon were also being troubled by false prophets; like those in Judah they were saying, "This captivity is not going to last very long. God is going to restore you. God will send you back to Judah." Jeremiah, hearing about this, writes them a letter, and this is the message he was given to deliver to them:

> "Thus says the Lord of hosts, the God of Israel, to all the exiles whom I have sent into exile from Jerusalem to Babylon: Build houses and live in them; plant gardens and eat their produce. Take wives and have sons and daughters; take wives for your sons, and give your daughters in marriage, that they may bear sons and daughters; multiply there, and do not decrease. But seek the welfare of the city where I have sent you into exile, and pray to the Lord on its behalf, for in its welfare you will find your welfare" (Jer. 29:4–7).

"You are going to be there a long time," God told them. "Settle down; accept it. Make the best of the situation, enjoy yourself while you are there to the fullest degree that you can. For remember, this is what I have chosen for you. It is the best way out. And while you are there, pray for Babylon, seek the welfare of Babylon."

Many of us may be in this same situation. Because of

resistance to the will and word of God in the past, we have been put in a situation we do not like very well, but we cannot change it. What does God say? "Accept it, work for the welfare of those around you. And wait for my time, for it will come."

> "For thus says the Lord: When seventy years are completed for Babylon, I will visit you, and I will fulfil to you my promise and bring you back to this place. For I know the plans I have for you, says the Lord, plans for welfare and not for evil, to give you a future and a hope. Then you will call upon me and come and pray to me, and I will hear you. You will seek me and find me; when you seek me with all your heart, I will be found by you . . ." (Jer. 29:10–14).

If you read the closing chapters of Daniel you will find that when Daniel was an old man, he realized as he read these very words in the prophecy of Jeremiah that God had fulfilled the seventy years of captivity. He had been a captive in Babylon for seventy years, and the time had come. Daniel obeyed this word and began to pray to God. And God gave him the great vision which closes that book, a vision which carried him on down through our own day to the end of time and showed him what would happen. And then God began to move the people of Israel to return to the land of Judah, as he had promised.

What Shall I Believe?

The closing words of the chapter are specific prophecies against certain false prophets among the exiles in Babylon. Their names are Ahab, Zedekiah, and Shemaiah. In verse 23, God says their names shall be cursed,

" '. . . because they have committed folly in
Israel, they have committed adultery with their
neighbors' wives, and they have spoken in my
name lying words which I did not command them.
I am the one who knows, and I am witness [i.e.,
"the one who speaks"], says the Lord.' "

This was a time of terrible uncertainty. People were torn
between many conflicting voices and rival factions, and
they didn't know what to believe. The supreme need of
the hour was that someone might know the facts and declare them, and thus give the people an indication of the
line of action to take. God says, "I am the one who knows.
I know what is going on in the inner lives of these people,
and I will make it known." That is the voice you can
trust.

God makes known his way, his will, and the truth in
three ways. First, in past history. In the light of Scriptures, we can see how God works in history; I would com-
mend to you the reading of it. History records all the
errors that we see around us today, as well as the solutions. No new error is introduced into the world which
has not already been answered in the record of the past.

Second, in current events; he is always bringing truth
to life. That is why we as a nation went through Watergate. Everything the most powerful men of our nation
thought they could keep hidden was forced into the light.
That is the way God works in the affairs of men.

And third, God makes the truth known through the
direct revelation of his Word, the truth as it is in Jesus,
coming to the man of God who speaks it out before the
people.

So in this day of confusion and uncertainty, which voice
will you listen to? The voices of the occult world around

us? The false prophets who are telling of visions which they claim to be coming from God? The secular voices which tell us that things are not the way the Bible says they are? Which voice will you listen to? Whom will you follow? What will be the guideline for your actions? Well, the message of Jeremiah is: "God rules in the affairs of men. And if you want to know how to behave now, listen to God, for he is the one who knows, and who makes all things known." Perhaps in a silent moment of meditation God would say something to you about your need to rethink some area of your life and adjust to the reality of his Word.

10

The Secret of Strength

In the Book of Jeremiah, chapters 30 through 33 constitute a trumpet note of hope and certainty arising out of the midst of deepest despair and distress. If you look at chapter 32 you will note that this section is dated in the tenth year of king Zedekiah. The captivity of Judah by Babylon took place in the eleventh year of his reign, so things are very close to the end. When we last saw our hero, Jeremiah, he was awaiting trial, under the indictment of the government for what they regarded as his treasonable activities against the king and the country, because he was recommending that people actually desert Jerusalem and give themselves up as captives to the Babylonians. We find Jeremiah now as a prisoner in the court of the guard. Nebuchadnezzar and his armies are at the gates of Jerusalem for the third time. The city has been under siege for over a year, and already sharp famine has set in. There is no bread in the city at all, and it appears to be only a matter of weeks before the city must capitulate to the siege of the Babylonian forces. There is no relief in sight, no one on the horizon to help them. The nation is facing perhaps the darkest hour in all its history. It is out of this darkness that chapters 30 and 31 arise.

They are part of what we might call "The Song of Jeremiah," a beautiful section of hope and confidence in the midst of despair and distress. Actually, it might be more accurate to call it "The Dream of Jeremiah." Martin Luther King was noted for a great speech in which, over and over, he said, "I have a dream," as he outlined the hopes and desires and longings of the black people in America. Jeremiah's song really *is* a dream, for in chapter 31, verse 26, a very strange statement is suddenly introduced. Jeremiah says, "Thereupon I awoke and looked, and my sleep was pleasant to me." Then he goes back again to the vision he is expounding. So this prophecy evidently came as a dream to Jeremiah in the night, a vision of the restoration and the glory God has promised his people.

But it is far more than that, because as you and I read through the account, we will see that this is the way God is working in our lives as well. God always works in the same way. He is a God who does not change. The revelation of the great purposes and programs of God in the Old Testament is given to us to show us what is happening to *us*.

Joyful Certainty

There are four themes in this song, blended and entwined together, but clearly distinguishable. The most dominant is the note of the *certainty of joy*, the feeling most often expressed in this song. Here is a sample:

> "And it shall come to pass in that day, says the Lord of hosts, that I will break the yoke from off their neck, and I will burst their bonds, and strangers shall no more make servants of them. But they shall serve the Lord their God and David

their king, whom I will raise up for them" (Jer. 30:8–9).

This passage looks far beyond the return from the Babylonian captivity and beyond our own day to the time when God promises to restore the fortunes of Israel, and even to raise up David to be king over the people again. Therefore, it is a promise not yet fulfilled. God is still waiting for this time.

Here is another beautiful expression of this joy to come:

"Therefore all who devour you shall be devoured,
　and all your foes, every one of them, shall go into captivity;
those who despoil you shall become a spoil,
　and all who prey on you I shall make a prey.
For I will restore health to you,
　and your wounds I will heal,
　　　　　　　　　says the Lord . . ." (Jer. 30:16–17).

All through the record of history it has been noteworthy that every nation which has attacked the Jews has found itself suffering as a result. God promises here to watch over his people, and to return evil upon those who harm them in any way. Further on he says,

"Thus says the Lord:
Behold, I will restore the fortunes of the tents of Jacob,
　and have compassion on his dwellings;
the city shall be rebuilt upon its mound,
　and the palace shall stand where it used to be.
Out of them shall come songs of thanksgiving,
　and the voices of those who make merry.
I will multiply them, and they shall not be few;
　I will make them honored, and they shall not be small.
Their children shall be as they were of old,
　and their congregation shall be established before me;
　and I will punish all who oppress them.

Their prince shall be one of themselves,
    their ruler shall come forth from their midst;
I will make him draw near, and he shall approach me,
    for who would dare of himself to approach me?
                      says the Lord.
And you shall be my people,
    and I will be your God" (Jer. 30:18–22).

It is evident that these words have never been fulfilled in all the history of Israel. In all the restorations they have gone through they have never come to anything like what is described here; so fulfillment awaits the future. There are many other passages—I am selecting only a few. Look at verses 7 and 8 of chapter 31:

For thus says the Lord:
"Sing aloud with gladness for Jacob,
    and raise shouts for the chief of the nations;
proclaim, give praise, and say,
    'The lord has saved his people,
    the remnant of Israel.'
Behold, I will bring them from the north country,
    and gather them from the farthest parts of the earth,
among them the blind and the lame,
    the woman with child and her who is in travail, together;
    a great company, they shall return here."

Many thought when Israel became a nation again, and Jews came from all parts of the earth back to the land of Israel, that this passage was thus fulfilled. But I do not think so. It was a foreview of it, as were other events in history. But it is not yet fully fulfilled, for at the present time they are not there in belief but in unbelief, whereas this passage speaks of their coming back in joy and worship. Look at verses 10 through 12:

"Hear the word of the Lord, O nations,
  and declare it in the coastlands afar off;
say, 'He who scattered Israel will gather him,
  and will keep him as a shepherd keeps his flock.'
For the Lord has ransomed Jacob,
  and has redeemed him from hands too strong for him.
They shall come and sing aloud on the height of Zion,
  and they shall be radiant over the goodness of the Lord,
over the grain, the wine, and the oil,
  and over the young of the flock and the herd;
their life shall be like a watered garden,
  and they shall languish no more."

Then verses 27 and 28:

> "Behold, the days are coming, says the Lord, when I will sow the house of Israel and the house of Judah with the seed of man and the seed of beast. And it shall come to pass that as I have watched over them to pluck up and break down, to overthrow, destroy, and bring evil, so I will watch over them to build and to plant, says the Lord."

The chapter closes with a very specific promise concerning the city of Jerusalem:

> "Behold, the days are coming, says the Lord, when the city shall be rebuilt for the Lord from the tower of Hananel to the Corner Gate. And the measuring line shall go out farther, straight to the hill Gareb, and shall then turn to Goah. The whole valley of the dead bodies and the ashes, and all the fields as far as the brook Kidron, to the corner of the Horse Gate toward the east, shall be sacred to the Lord. It shall not be uprooted or overthrown any more for ever" (Jer. 31:38–40).

That encompasses practically the whole city of old Jerusalem at the present time. It is obvious that this too is yet to be fulfilled. But what a scene of beauty and glory, what a promise of joy and of gladness, after centuries of wandering and sorrow! And notice when this promise is given. It is when these people were at the lowest stage of their national life. They were a wanton, wicked, and wayward people, stubborn and rebellious. God had been dealing with them in faithfulness for many, many centuries, trying to turn them around. It had been four hundred years since the days of David and the height of the nation's power and glory. Now, despite occasional reforms, they have sunk lower and lower until, in stubborn determination to have their own way, they are now about to be carried away into captivity in Babylon, Jerusalem is to be leveled by the Babylonian forces, and all their national glory is to perish. By every human reckoning, the state of this nation is absolutely hopeless. Nothing can be done for them. And yet in the midst of that darkness comes this great song of certainty and joy. God promises that he is going to save this people, to change them, and that they will return in the beautiful way described here. That is the dominant note of this song, and it is one of the most beautiful series of passages of Scripture.

Like Women in Labor

Closely mingled with this is another theme—quite a different one—the *agony of distress*. In fact, this vision is introduced on that note:'

These are the words which the Lord spoke concerning Israel and Judah:
"Thus says the Lord:

We have heard a cry of panic,
    of terror, and no peace,
Ask now, and see,
    can a man bear a child?
Why then do I see every man
    with his hands on his loins like a woman in labor?
    Why has every face turned pale?
Alas! that day is so great
    there is none like it;
it is a time of distress for Jacob;
    yet he shall be saved out of it" (Jer. 30:4–7).

These words remind us of what Jesus said: "For then there will be great tribulation, such as has not been from the beginning of the world until now, no, and never will be" (Matt. 24:21). And here, in Jeremiah's vivid figure, the men are seen gripping themselves like women in labor, in agony and pain and terror, as this day advances. The Lord says, "It is a time of distress for Jacob." We know that this is yet to come.

The Scriptures make very clear that any peace Israel may make with its neighbors will not last; sooner or later it will be broken again. The time of Jacob's trouble is yet ahead, and it will be a time of great distress, worse than they have ever seen before. Now, when you think of the holocaust in which six million Jews were murdered in the gas chambers of the Nazis, you can hardly imagine what this upcoming time could be like, when it is said to be as no other in all the history of Israel. But God is careful to point out the reason for it:

Why do you cry out over your hurt?
Your pain is incurable.

> Because your guilt is great,
>> because your sins are flagrant,
>> I have done these things to you (Jer. 30:15).

God takes the full responsibility for what happens to Israel. He says, "I have brought it to pass." It is as though he stands with his hands on his hips and says to them, "Look, I'm responsible. Any questions?" He says that it is because of their sins, their *flagrant* sins.

Inevitable Consequences

We must not read this as though it were something remote from us. If you are inclined to say only, "Oh, it's such a pity what's going to happen to Israel," remember that this is your story, too. This is the way God works. He deals with Israel this way because this is the way he deals with everybody. There is a scriptural principle reflected here which we all too often forget. Paul said very plainly in Galatians 6:7–8, "Do not be deceived [i.e., don't kid yourself]; God is not mocked." Just because judgment does not fall immediately upon people they think they have gotten by. But Paul says, "Don't fool yourself; God is not cheated. Whatever a man sows, that he will also reap. For he who sows to his own flesh will from the flesh reap corruption [i.e., trouble, pain, heartache, trial, distress, and disaster] . . ." Now, that is inevitable. God does not cancel that out by the forgiveness of sin. That is part of what we call the natural consequences of evil, or the temporal judgment of God. That is inevitable, but so is the rest of what Paul says: ". . . but he who sows to the Spirit will from the Spirit reap eternal life." The joy and glory of life—not just in heaven someday, but now—will come to us if we walk in the Spirit, and that, too, is inevitable.

Now, the temporal judgment that I referred to means, of course, that ultimately a recompense comes to us in this life for the evil in which we have indulged our flesh—whether it is blatant, open, sensual evil, or inward evil, such as spiritual pride, bitterness, and all the other sins of the spirit. It makes no difference; evil brings its own results. As someone has well said, "You can pull out the nail driven into the wall, but you can't pull out the nail hole." God reminds us here that there will be pain, heartache, and trouble because of the evil of our past. The sins of our youth will catch up to us—usually in middle age! As Kipling has said, "The sins that they did two by two, they pay for one by one." God said this is inevitable for his people Israel, and it is inevitable for us as well.

But now there is a very necessary third note struck in this song, which is blended together with the others—the *faithfulness of love.* Look at the first few verses of chapter 31:

> "At that time, says the Lord, I will be the God
> of all the families of Israel, and they shall be my
> people."
> Thus says the Lord:
> "The people who survived the sword
>   found grace in the wilderness;
> when Israel sought for rest,
>   the Lord appeared to him from afar."

"I will be with you in the middle of the trouble," he says. "You will have to go through it, but you do not have to go alone; there will be grace and love to sustain you."

"I have loved you with an everlasting love;
    therefore I have continued my faithfulness to you" (Jer. 31:3).

I want to return in a moment and comment on this quality of God's love, but first let's look at a couple of other passages. Verse 9:

"With weeping they shall come,
    and with consolations I will lead them back,
I will make them walk by brooks of water,
    in a straight path in which they shall not stumble;
for I am a father to Israel,
    and Ephraim is my first-born."

Here is the Father's love which is behind this entire scene. Then verse 20:

"Is Ephraim my dear son?
    Is he my darling child?
For as often as I speak against him,
    I do remember him still.
Therefore my heart yearns for him;
    I will surely have mercy on him,"

says the Lord.

Love Without Dimension

As a father whose heart is tender toward his son—no matter how sharply he must reprimand him—so God is tender toward his people. And behind the darkness and the distress is the everlasting love of God. In this beautiful phrase, "I have loved you with an everlasting love," the word *everlasting* is one of those words which baffle us. We hardly know what it means. Even in the original language it is difficult to define. *Everlasting* connotes more than duration, means more than merely "eternal"; it has in it an element of mystery. That is, it refers literally to the "vanishing point." Let your mind run back into the past over all the years of history, and you come to a place where finally you just cannot think any further. Yet logic affirms that even beyond this point there has been existence and time, so this is the vanishing point. And this is what *everlasting* means. Let your mind run into the future, and you come to the same kind of haziness, a place where you no longer can comprehend what the ages mean, where times and durations seem meaningless. That, again, is the vanishing point in the future, beyond which lie experiences for God's people, but which we are unable to grasp. That is the mystery of this word, *everlasting*. It is a word which means "beyond dimension," "greater than we can think." This is what Paul is expressing in Ephesians: ". . . that you, being rooted and grounded in love, may have power to comprehend with all the saints what is the breadth and length and height and depth, and to know the love of Christ which surpasses knowledge . . ." (Eph. 3:17*b*–19*a*).

So when you get to the place where the sins of the past, and those of your mothers and fathers before you, are taking their toll upon your life, and you are tempted to cry out and say, "Why? Why should this happen to me? What have I done to deserve this?" (It is remarkable how short our memories are, how we think of ourselves only in terms of what we are now, while God remembers all that we have been. We forget all that and we think it is "unjust" of God to treat us the way he does.) When this happens, God is at pains to remind us that what we are experiencing is his everlasting love, his mysterious love.

That is, he is saying to us, "Look, it may pain you, but it won't damage you. This very hurt you are going through is what will produce in you the character that both you and I want. It is this which will mellow you, refine you, soften you, open you up, make you a human being. Instead of a hard, callous, resistant, self-centered

person, you'll become open and responsive and selfless."
That is what God is saying. That is the mysterious quality of this love which draws us on. "I have loved you with
an everlasting love; therefore I have continued my faithfulness to you," he says. "I have not let you miss out on a
thing which is a result of the exercise of the flesh in your
life." That sounds strange to us, does it not? We want to
escape the consequences, but instead, God leads us
through them.

A New Covenant

This brings us to the last note of this song, a remarkable one—the discovery of a *new way:*

> "Behold, the days are coming, says the Lord,
> when I will make a new covenant with the house
> of Israel and the house of Judah, not like the
> covenant which I made with their fathers when I
> took them by the hand to bring them out of the
> land of Egypt, my covenant which they broke,
> though I was their husband, says the Lord. But
> this is the covenant which I will make with the
> house of Israel after those days, says the Lord:
> I will put my law within them, and I will write it
> upon their hearts; and I will be their God, and they
> shall be my people. And no longer shall each man
> teach his neighbor and each his brother, saying,
> 'Know the Lord,' for they shall all know me, from
> the least of them to the greatest, says the Lord; for
> I will forgive their iniquity, and I will remember
> their sin no more" (Jer. 31:31–34).

This is a marvelous promise, a promise that God is going
to do what the people themselves could never do. Despite
all their failure, and all their vain efforts to do what God
wanted, he will bring them around. And he will do it by

a new process, a process which has three simple manifestations.

First, he says, "I will put my law within them, and I will write it upon their hearts." That is a new *motive*. God is going to change the motivation of a person's life, so that it will come from within instead of without. The Old Covenant, the Law, is a demand made on us from without. "Do this, and I'll do that," says God. This proves to be impossible for man to carry out. But the New Covenant is something put within us. What is it? Love. Love becomes the motive in the New Covenant. It is the motive for life—to respond out of love for God, out of love for what he has already done in our life and heart. As love is built within us, as we understand and realize the glory of a relationship with a living God, love is our response. And it is on the basis of love that God then asks for obedience. "Love," says the Apostle Paul, "is the fulfilling of the Law." No man can harm his neighbor who first loves him.

The second manifestation is a new *power*. "I will be their God, and they shall be my people." That is, God himself is the strength of man's life. He supplies all the power to act. We are the ones who do the acting; he is the One who does the supplying. This is a beautiful description of the New Covenant; everything coming from God; nothing coming from me. God is at work in me. That is the new power.

Then there is a new *family*. "And no longer shall each man teach his neighbor and each his brother, saying, 'Know the Lord,' for they shall all know me, from the least of them to the greatest, says the Lord." "They will all know me"—isn't that marvelous? We all have but one Father because we are one family. All those in the family know each other. All we have to do is find out each other's names! We already know what are the dominant drives, and underlying hopes and passions of each life, because they are all basically the same: that we might know him better, become like him. That is why, when Christians meet one another, though they have never met before, and may be from opposite sides of the globe, they always have a ground of sharing—right from the start. They know each other, know the same Lord, share the same life. And that is why they can help one another.

Not long ago I was up in northern Minnesota amid the birch trees and lakes, not far from the Canadian border. I was with a group of pastors and their wives in a conference. These were wonderful people, but they were inhibited, not free. I taught on the New Covenant all week long, not from this passage, but from the New Testament. At the end of the meeting we had a service in which I invited them to share their difficulties and to help bear one another's burdens as part of the family of God. They were reluctant to do so, even as pastors, and their sharing was very superficial. They talked about some ordinary victories and joys, and a few very minor problems—like the need for a new mimeograph machine. Finally I stopped them and said, "Look, you're going to go back as pastors wanting to teach your congregations how to share, and you're not sharing yourselves. You're not opening up your hurts and your hearts." And I urged them to do so.

A young man stood up and told about how he and his wife had returned from Brazil where they had been missionaries for three years. They had returned with a deep sense of failure, and had been resentful of others who had not understood what had gone on in their lives. Then a young woman stood up and told how her young husband, a pastor, had died the year before, and how lonely her life had been, how empty it was. She said, "I know you can't meet my needs like my husband did, but I just ask you to pray for me." People began to weep and to pray for one another. A man stood up and said that he and his wife had been going through a terrible time of distress because their daughter had died. No one had known that they were going through this, and this was the first time they were able to share their feelings. Then a man stood up and confessed his sin of judgmental criticism against a woman who was present, and asked her forgiveness. They forgave one another. Another woman stood up and shared how jealous she had been of her husband's ministry, and how wrong she knew this was. She realized that this was a sin in her own life, and asked for forgiveness. Soon they were sharing with one another out of their depths. Tears were running down their faces, and they were really praying and upholding one another. I finally just sat down. The Lord was running the meeting, and he did not need me. We ended with a communion service in which many were feeling healed, restored, cleansed! As they passed the cup to one another, they would say, "Your sins are forgiven you." It was the New Covenant in action.

Provision for Failure

You see, the basis for this New Covenant is given in the final words of this section. It all rests on this great platform: ". . . for I will forgive their iniquity, and I will remember their sin no more" (Jer. 31:34). That is how God proposes to win this battle. When the Law, with its demands, fails, and we cannot respond the way we know we ought to, how are we going to win? When the case is hopeless, how is it going to be changed? Well, as God says here, it is changed when we begin to understand that provision has already been fully made for all our failure. God does not hold failure against us. His love will be with us and will sustain us even through the results of our folly and our failure. He does not hold anything against us; he is for us, and with us in it, and will turn all the difficulty we are going through to our own advantage, so that it brings us out beautiful people—softened, helped, healed. That is the New Covenant in action. That is the way God does it. As we learn more and more to walk in dependence upon a new motive and a new power, in a new relationship with one another, resting upon the forgiveness of God, we discover that marvelous things are happening in our life.

Some day, historically, God is going to soften and heal Israel. Stubborn and willful as they are (and they themselves admit they are among the stubbornest people on the face of the earth), yet God will bring them around, to understand the New Covenant relationship they have with him. This will occur to Israel sometime in the future. Spiritually, that healing relationship with God has been available to all men for centuries—ever since man first appeared on the earth. This blood of the New Covenant has been shed before the foundation of the world, Scripture tells us, so that man might come to God on this basis, and this alone. But here God guarantees that he is going to bring Israel into this kind of relationship. Look at these words in verses 35 and 36:

Thus says the Lord,
who gives the sun for light by day
    and the fixed order of the moon and stars for light by night,
who stirs up the sea so that its waves roar—
    the Lord of hosts is his name:
"If this fixed order departs
    from before me, says the Lord,

then shall the descendants of Israel cease
    from being a nation before me for ever."

Do you think Israel is in danger of being wiped out? No, nothing can wipe out this nation. As long as the sun is in the sky, or the moon comes up at night, or the seasons come through the years, God will never allow his people to be wiped out. Never! He promises that this cannot happen, unless the very natural order of the universe be destroyed first. And furthermore,

Thus says the Lord:
"If the heavens above can be measured,
    and the foundations of the earth below can be explored,
then I will cast off all the descendants of Israel
    for all that they have done,
                    says the Lord" (Jer. 31:35–37).

That is, he guarantees that one of these days he will open their eyes and they will understand, and will turn again as a people. And Israel shall fill the earth and be the head of the nations, as God has promised, and David their king shall rule over them. Days of glory and joy shall come back again to earth. For as Paul argues in the eleventh chapter of Romans, if the temporary rejection of Israel meant riches and joy and grace to us, how much more will their full inclusion mean, the salvation of this people, when they come at last into their promise. And just as he has made it sure to them, so he makes it sure to us. This is *our* promise; we too rest upon the New Covenant.

When Jesus sat down with his disciples in the upper room the night before the crucifixion, he took the bread and the cup, and he passed the bread among them, saying, "This is my body which is given for you." Then he passed the cup and said, "This cup is the blood of the new covenant." God has made that covenant with any who are ready to come to him, who have reached the end of themselves, who have stopped trying to do it themselves, and are resting on what he is ready to do. That is why the Sermon on the Mount begins with the bankruptcy of humanity: "Blessed are the poor in spirit, for theirs is the kingdom of heaven." Out of our bankruptcy comes God's full supply. That is the New Covenant.

11

Is Anything Too Hard for God?

In our study from Jeremiah we will see now something of the greatness and the weakness of faith. True faith is both great and weak—and we want to examine that paradox. Chapters 32 and 33 are the second part of the great song of hope that Jeremiah sang when he was shut up in the court of the guard at the order of king Zedekiah. This section of the song is introduced by another of the remarkable series of visual aids with which God instructed, taught, and toughened this prophet. God is always in the business of preparing us for trials yet to come. Somehow the idea has spread abroad that life ought to be delightful and free from trouble. And we feel short-changed if our experience is anything other than that. Yet the Scriptures tell us over and over that this is not the way it is going to be. We cannot live free of trouble with the world in its present condition—under the domination of Satan, the god of this world. But God will use that trouble in our lives, and he toughens us to meet it, just as he did with Jeremiah. I do not think anything about this book has helped me more than to see how God worked with this prophet to strengthen his faith and to help him

171

meet his trials. Let's begin reading with verse 6, where we have the story of what the Lord asked Jeremiah to do:

> Jeremiah said, "The word of the Lord came to me: Behold, Hanamel the son of Shallum your uncle will come to you and say, 'Buy my field which is at Anathoth, for the right of redemption by purchase is yours.' Then Hanamel my cousin came to me in the court of the guard, in accordance with the word of the Lord, and said to me, 'Buy my field which is at Anathoth in the land of Benjamin, for the right of possession and redemption is yours; buy it for yourself.' Then I knew that this was the word of the Lord.
>
> "And I bought the field at Anathoth from Hanamel my cousin, and weighed out the money to him, seventeen shekels of silver. I signed the deed, sealed it, got witnesses, and weighed the money on scales" (Jer. 32:6–10).

That is a remarkable act of faith, for it was the worst possible time to be buying property in Judah. Jerusalem was under immediate threat of capture by the Babylonian army and the entire land would be subjected to at least seventy years of desolation and darkness and despair. And yet God sent Jeremiah word to buy this field in his hometown of Anathoth. Though Jeremiah was shut up in the court of the guard, God told him his cousin would come to him. When he came and offered the field, Jeremiah was to buy it.

Qualities of Faith

That wonderful act of faith belongs, in my judgment, with those acts of faith in the incomplete record of Hebrews 11. As we examine it, we will learn, in practical ways, what it means to walk by faith. Every one of us is called to walk by faith in these days, and there are certain essential and unmistakable qualities of faith revealed here. First there is what we might call "the *caution* of faith." Notice how the account progressed. God said to Jeremiah, in the loneliness of his prison, "Your cousin Hanamel is coming to you, offering to sell his field." A little later on the account says, "Then Hanamel my cousin came to me . . . *in accordance* with the word of the Lord." Later still, "Then I knew this *was* the word of the Lord." The important thing to see is how Jeremiah tested this impression he received.

Many of us have wondered how these Old Testament prophets were given "words" from God. Many times you find this phrase in the Scriptures: "The word of the Lord came to me . . ." People have asked me, "How did it come? Did God thunder with a loud and audible voice?" Sometimes he did, but that was not the usual way. This account suggests that the usual way God spoke to these prophets was the same way he speaks to us, that is, through a vivid impression made upon the soul, an inner voice saying something, directing us somewhere, informing us of something. We have all had this experience. We know what this inner voice is like. But the great lesson to learn from this account is that *this inner voice is not always the voice of God.* Sometimes the god of this world can speak through that inner voice, sounding very much like the voice of God. Many a person has been tremendously injured in his faith, and has damaged the faith of others, by acting impulsively on what this inner voice has to say, without testing whether it is the voice of God or not.

You notice that faith here, though it acts in a remarkable way, does not act fanatically. Faith is never fanati-

cal; it acts cautiously, expecting God to confirm his word.
Jeremiah was no novice in the active life of faith. He
knew that God would confirm his word, and he had
learned to wait upon God. God confirmed the word by
fulfilling the prediction he had made. Sometimes he con-
firms it in other ways. Scripture gives us a great principle
we all ought to remember: "In the mouth of two or three
witnesses every word shall be established." Look for those
two or three witnesses before you act upon an inner voice,
for God will confirm it to you. This inner voice told Jeremiah what would happen, but he did not act then; he
waited until it was confirmed by the coming of Hanamel.

I know of a dear Christian girl who, with all the ear-
nestness of her heart, and desiring to know and follow
God, felt that God had placed an impression in her heart
that she should marry a certain man. She did not know
him very well, nor was she in love with him, but she felt
certain that this was the voice of God—so certain that she
began to anticipate ways and means by which this might
come to pass. But in the course of a few months, to her
dismay and consternation, this young man announced his
engagement to another girl. She was dismayed not because she was in love with him, because she wasn't, but
because she was so certain she had heard the voice of God.
It turned out that he did marry this other girl, and she was
troubled, wondering how she could have been so misled.
Later on she felt that another word, this time concerning
her parents, had been given to her, but this did not work
out either. Gradually she learned the great fact that Jeremiah tells us here: it is necessary to act with caution
about an inner voice, and to expect God to confirm his
word to us, so that we may act with understanding.

Yet, along with all the caution of faith, another quality

of faith is very apparent in this account. It is what we might call "the *audacity* of faith." It was thoroughly unreasonable, even ridiculous, to buy property when the city was about to fall into enemy hands. But faith often has an apparent ridiculousness about it. You are not acting by faith if you are doing what everyone around you is doing. Faith often appears to defy the circumstances; it constitutes a risk and a venture.

In Hebrews 11 we are told that Noah built an ark where there was no water, and when there had never been any rain. I am sure the people of his day called him Crazy Noah—building an ark out on the dry land! Abraham went on a journey without a map. People asked him, "Where are you going?" He said, "We don't know; we're just going, that's all. God is leading us." They must have twirled their fingers alongside their heads and said, "Poor Abe—he's lost his marbles!" Moses forsook the treasures and wisdom of Egypt, that he might go out and wander in the desert with a rabble who had nothing. People must have said, "He's crazy!" That is the quality of faith—it acts in an apparently ridiculous way. But it acts this way because it is based on a higher knowledge. It always has a certain basis on which to rest. Therefore faith does not demand that we run out and do foolish, impulsive acts, without any reason. The reason is higher than many people can see, but it is there.

I doubt if Hanamel was acting by faith. He was simply taking advantage of the situation. He saw a chance to unload his property before the city fell. You can take money with you into captivity, but you cannot take land. My mind goes back to the days shortly after the outbreak of World War II. Along with about two thousand other young men, I was on a troop transport on the way to

Hawaii from San Francisco. We were convoyed by two American destroyers, guarding against attack by Japanese submarines. Sure enough, about three-quarters of the way across, the general alarm sounded one morning. All passengers aboard were put down in the hold. The destroyers dropped depth charges, and they did indeed sink a submarine. We heard the terrible clang as these depth charges exploded and the concussion banged against the side of our vessel. About a thousand men were gathered in the hold where I was, and we wondered what was going to happen. It was a very tense and quiet time, until suddenly the tension was broken by a voice crying out, "Does anybody want to buy a good watch?" I thought of that when I read this account of Hanamel wanting to sell his property to Jeremiah. That is how ridiculous it was. But God was in it. And faith is willing to look ridiculous, because it is based upon a higher knowledge.

No Halfway Measures

That leads to the third element, which we can call "the *commitment* of faith":

> "Then I took the sealed deed of purchase, containing the terms and conditions, and the open copy; and I gave the deed of purchase to Baruch the son of Neriah son of Mahseiah, in the presence of Hanamel my cousin, in the presence of the witnesses who signed the deed of purchase, and in the presence of all the Jews who were sitting in the court of the guard. I charged Baruch in their presence, saying, 'Thus says the Lord of hosts, the God of Israel: Take these deeds, both this sealed deed of purchase and this open deed, and put them in an earthenware vessel, that they may last for a long time. For thus says the Lord of

hosts, the God of Israel: Houses and fields and
vineyards shall again be bought in this land'"
(Jer. 32:11–15).

What a ringing testimony to the power and greatness of
God! This was not a hopeless condition. God had said the
land would ultimately be restored, and this deed would be
valid. Therefore, it was to be put in a safe place. But the
remarkable thing here is that Jeremiah conformed to
normal procedures. Again I stress, faith is not fanatical—
not really. It appears to be, to those who do not understand the full situation, because faith is based upon a
higher knowledge; it is therefore thorough and consistent
in its obedience. It conforms to accepted procedures, and
works through normal channels, and makes everything
public and open to examination by anyone interested.

Accordingly, Jeremiah sent Baruch down to the title
company and had him bring a deed to be signed. He acted
before witnesses, and had the witnesses sign the deed and
the copy—both to be sealed in a safe deposit box, so that
eventually his heirs might claim title to this land. He
worked in this normal way, and then clearly announced
the purpose of it all: "It is because God says that houses
and fields and vineyards will be bought in this land
again."

Faith takes no halfway measures. When it begins to
act, it acts completely, consistently, and all the way.
There is no hedging of Jeremiah's bets here, no saying to
these people, "Well, I'm just buying this property on
speculation, hoping it will all work out, but it's just a
gamble, a shot in the dark." No, he assures them that God
has spoken, and that everything he is doing is consistent
with the word of God.

So far we have seen that faith is audacious, but faith

is also cautious, waiting upon the word of God. And faith is consistent and committed in its actions. But now one more quality of faith is revealed in this account. Beginning with verse 16 and continuing through verse 25, a remarkable prayer of Jeremiah is recorded. These are Jeremiah's private thoughts about this deed. Before men this prophet is bold and resolute and confident. But before God he admits that he is not quite so sure this is all going to work out. I am glad this account is here, because this is what we might call "the *doubtings* of faith."

The Proof of Faith

Faith always has its doubts. As a young Christian, I had the impression that if you doubted, you could not have faith; that faith and doubt were contrary to one another, and doubt was the opposite of faith. But I gradually began to understand that this is not true. Doubt is the proof of faith. Doubt is an attack upon faith. You cannot have doubts unless you have faith. Faith is the way God works, and so the enemy is bound to attack your faith immediately as he sees you beginning to act and live and walk by faith. Therefore doubts will begin to arise—as a result of Satan's attempt to overthrow your faith. I have learned that there is no faith without doubts.

We can establish the fact that Jesus himself, though he *always* lived by faith and everything he did was by faith, nevertheless was subjected to times of severe doubt. Otherwise he was not "one who in every respect has been tempted as we are, yet without sinning." Doubt is part of the life of faith. If you are trying to walk by faith in a promise God has given you, and you are troubled by doubts, I say to you that this is the proof you are really living by faith. Hang in there! Do not let your doubts overthrow you.

Look at this prayer; Jeremiah begins by reminding himself of the character of God:

> "After I had given the deed of purchase to Baruch the son of Neriah, I prayed to the Lord, saying, 'Ah Lord God! It is thou who hast made the heavens and the earth by thy great power and by thy outstretched arm! Nothing is too hard for thee, who showest steadfast love to thousands, but dost requite the guilt of fathers to their children after them, O great and mighty God whose name is the Lord of hosts, great in counsel and mighty in deed; whose eyes are open to all the ways of men, rewarding every man according to his ways and according to the fruit of his doings; who hast shown signs and wonders in the land of Egypt, and to this day in Israel and among all mankind, and hast made thee a name, as at this day' " (Jer. 32:16–20).

What is Jeremiah doing? He is following the pattern of prayer that Jesus himself taught us. Jesus said, "When you pray, this is the way to do it. Begin here: 'Our Father who art in heaven, hallowed be thy name.' Remind yourself of the name of God, the greatness of his being, and the faithfulness of his character." This is what Jeremiah is doing. He starts off by reminding himself of the God of power who made the heavens and the earth—nothing is too hard for him; of the God of faithful love, who both saves and judges men; of the God of wisdom and truth, whom history reveals, who has done great wonders among mankind, and whose wonders stand embedded in history. No one can disprove them. That is the kind of God he is. Jeremiah is strengthening himself by the greatness of his God, because of the ferocity of the attack upon his faith. He goes on to recount the history of Israel, to remember how God has worked with his people, and to remark the accuracy of God's predictions. Then he brings it right down to his present hour:

> " 'Behold the siege mounds have come up to the city to take it, and because of sword and famine and pestilence the city is given into the hands of the Chaldeans who are fighting against it. What thou didst speak has come to pass, and behold, thou seest it' " (vs. 24).

"There it is, Lord. There's Nebuchadnezzar with his great armies, and their fearsome reputation for cruelty, right outside the walls. Here's the city about to fall. Lord, it has come to pass—just as you said." But notice. Jeremiah is aware of God, and he is trying to strengthen his faith by these means. He has recounted the history of his people. This is the way he should pray. He began by affirming that nothing is too hard for God. And yet when he comes right down to his present experience, the very present hour, his faith trembles. He closes with these words: " 'Yet thou, O Lord God, hast said to me, "Buy the field for money and get witnesses"— . . .' " The Revised Standard Version correctly places a dash there, as though he had to pause, hardly able to go on. Finally he continues, " '. . . —though the city is given into the hands of the Chaldeans' " (vs. 25). And that is the end of his prayer. You see, his faith is trembling. The situation looks impossible. He began by affirming, "Nothing is too hard for thee"; he ends by suggesting, "Lord, this may be it! I don't see how you're going to handle this one!"

Now, his problem is not the desolation of the city; it is the degradation of the people. I don't think Jeremiah worried a bit about God's ability to rebuild and restore the city. The thing that constituted a tremendous dilemma to him was that the city could not be restored unless *the people* were changed and cleansed and healed. Remember, this man had been preaching to these people for forty years. For forty years he had poured out his heart to this people, declaring to them again and again the word of the Lord. And for forty years he had seen absolutely no sign of repentance—nobody turned, nobody stopped, nobody changed. The kings all refused his testimony. And though God faithfully supported his prophet again and again by causing his words to come to pass, nevertheless this people stubbornly resisted. Jeremiah says, "I don't see how you can change them, God. They're too stubborn." Is that not often our problem? We say, "Oh, the person I expected to see changed is too stubborn. There's no way he can change."

Look at God's reply to this dilemma of faith. God gives Jeremiah a tremendously detailed answer, beginning by reaffirming his power and his intentions for Jerusalem:

> The word of the Lord came to Jeremiah [at this point in his prayer]: "Behold, I am the Lord, the God of all flesh; is anything too hard for me? Therefore, thus says the Lord: Behold, I am giving this city into the hands of the Chaldeans and into the hand of Nebuchadrezzar king of Babylon, and he shall take it" (Jer. 32:26–28).

"Is anything too hard for me?" God's word echoes Jeremiah's own phrase as he began this prayer! This is what

God said to Sarah when she laughed in the tent of Abraham at God's promise that she would have a son. She knew her body was past childbearing, so she laughed. God said, "Why do you laugh? Is anything too hard for the Lord?" Though Scripture does not tell us this, I think Sarah had a little plaque made and put up right over the kitchen sink. And every time she did the dishes she looked at it: "Is anything too hard for the Lord?" The New Testament tells us that she was a woman of faith. And when Isaac was born she named him "Laughter," because it was so funny to think back to that day when she laughed at God, and he had said, "Is anything too hard for me?"

This is what God says to Jeremiah: "Is anything too hard for me?" And he prefaces it with these words: "I am the Lord, the God of *all* flesh." I do not know about you, but my problem often is that, while I'm fairly confident God can work with Christians, nonbelievers seem to be so hard and stubborn and resistant that he cannot do much with them. That was Jeremiah's problem. But God reminds him, "Look, I am the God of *all* flesh. I specialize in people—especially difficult people! Difficult people are my special stock in trade. Is anything too hard for me?"

Help My Unbelief

Then at the close of this chapter he goes on and reviews the sin of Israel, and reaffirms, in a passage of infinite beauty—which I hope you will read at your leisure—his ultimate intention to heal the hurt of Jerusalem. He says again to Jeremiah, "Jeremiah, this is what I'm going to do: I'll heal this city, I'll restore it and bring it back." But Jeremiah still is struggling, and so the opening words of chapter 33 tell us that the word of the Lord came a second time. God comes back to his troubled prophet with further information, and at this point invites him to inquire further:

> The word of the Lord came to Jeremiah a second time, while he was still shut up in the court of the guard: "Thus says the Lord who made the earth, the Lord who formed it to establish it [There is a record of achievement, if you like: he said he'd make it, and he did; he said he'd establish it, and he did.]—the Lord is his name: Call to me and I will answer you, and will tell you great and hidden things which you have not known" (Jer. 33:1–3).

There is something wonderfully helpful about that to me. God is saying here, in effect, that the man who takes his unbelief to God is the one who will be invited by God to enter into the secrets of the Almighty. Our problem is that we take our unbelief to each other. We are always complaining that God does not fulfill his word. I know we are not that bald-faced about it, but that is what we are really saying. When we say, "Well, this doesn't work for me," it means God is a respecter of persons; he only does it for a certain favored few—even though he says he is not that kind of God. Or somebody will say, "Well, you may have faith enough to believe that, but I don't understand it that way at all. It's all in the way you interpret it." That is really a cop-out. It is the same as saying, "I don't believe God is going to do it." We take our unbelief to each other, and that is why our faith does not grow.

But the man or woman of faith takes his or her unbelief to God, and lays the struggle before him. "God, I know you're this kind of a God, but I can't see how you're

going to do this!" And God honors that. There is record
after record in the Scripture of men and women who have
struggled like this, who have taken their doubts and their
unbelief and laid them before God. And never once is
there a single suggestion that he ever rebuked them for
that. There was that troubled father in the Gospels who
asked Jesus to heal his demonically oppressed son. Jesus
said, "According to your faith be it so." The man said,
"I believe; help my unbelief." Jesus immediately spoke
and delivered his son. And Jeremiah brought his unbelief
to the Lord, and so the Lord said, "Call to me, ask me,
and I will answer you, and will tell you the great and
hidden things which you don't understand."

Beginning with verse 4, God outlines the process he is
going to follow in bringing his promises about, giving
Jeremiah the details. Then he outlines the power by
which it is going to happen. And finally, he guarantees it
by the processes of nature. Notice the program that God
now unfolds to him. First, it will be destruction that leads
to cleansing:

> "For thus says the Lord, the God of Israel, con-
> cerning the houses of this city and the houses of
> the kings of Judah which were torn down to make
> a defense against the siege mounds and before
> the sword: The Chaldeans are coming in to fight
> and to fill them with the dead bodies of men whom
> I shall smite in my anger and my wrath, for I have
> hidden my face from this city because of all their
> wickedness" (Jer. 33:4–5).

Destruction is often God's first step, because we have
been building on a false foundation, and God knows he
must destroy what we have thought was true before he
can finally cleanse us. Many of us could testify of the hour

when God broke down everything we were counting on, shattering our expectations, and disappointing our dreams, and we were stricken. And in that hour we began to look at ourselves anew, and saw how much we had been contributing to the problem, blaming it on everybody else. That was the hour when God cleansed us. Cleansing is part of restoration, but destruction is necessary to cleansing.

The next revelation is that cleansing leads to joy:

> "I will cleanse them from all the guilt of their sin against me, and I will forgive all the guilt of their sin and rebellion against me. And this city shall be to me a name of joy, a praise and a glory before all the nations of the earth who shall hear of all the good that I do for them . . ." (vss. 8–9).

The great thing to remember in all of God's process with us is that his purpose in our lives, in everything that happens to us, is to increase our joy. You cannot read the Scriptures without seeing that his intention for men is that men should live in a continual sense of joy, of peace, of mirth and merriment and gladness of heart. That is what he has in mind, and he knows the steps it takes to bring it about.

Finally, joy permits prosperity:

> "Thus says the Lord of hosts: In this place which is waste, without man or beast, and in all of its cities, there shall again be habitations of shepherds resting their flocks. In the cities of the hill country, in the cities of the Shephelah, and in the cities of the Negeb, in the land of Benjamin, the places about Jerusalem, and in the cities of Judah, flocks shall again pass under the hands of the one who counts them, says the Lord" (Jer. 33:12–13).

That is a picture of prosperous conditions—the country-side filled with shepherds and their flocks—a beautiful picture. What God is saying is that the only time it is safe for us to be prosperous is when we have been cleansed and brought to joy. We are always trying to short-circuit God and leap ahead, to forget the intervening steps and to become prosperous. Prosperity never abides unless it is based upon joyful people who know how to live together in love. That is why God will withhold ultimate prosperity until that time.

The City of Gold

Then he takes the prophet a step further still, and in a great passage of light and glory he reveals the power that will accomplish this:

> "Behold, the days are coming, says the Lord, when I will fulfil the promise I made to the house of Israel and the house of Judah. In those days and at that time I will cause a righteous Branch to spring forth for David; and he shall execute justice and righteousness in the land. In those days Judah will be saved and Jerusalem will dwell securely. And this is the name by which it ["she"—in the Hebrew it is a feminine pronoun, referring to the city] will be called: 'The Lord is our righteousness.' [Literally, simply "The Lord, our righteousness."]
>
> "For thus says the Lord: David shall never lack a man to sit on the throne of the house of Israel, and the Levitical priests shall never lack a man in my presence to offer burnt offerings, to burn cereal offerings, and to make sacrifices for ever" (Jer. 33:14–18).

God would always have a king after the line of David, and a priest after the order of Mechizedek. As we know, in the course of time that man came: Jesus, the King who is our righteousness, whose righteousness is imparted to us—"The Lord, our righteousness." In chapter 23, verses 5 and 6, Jeremiah had referred to this very thing. But there the wording was, ". . . *he* will be called: 'The Lord is our righteousness.' " Here God says of the city, ". . . she will be called: 'The Lord, our righteousness.' " By this he indicates that we, who become the city of God, the new Jerusalem, are made to partake of the very righteousness of Christ our Lord.

In fact, the entire restoration is going to be characterized by this one word: *righteousness*. Righteousness consists, first of all, of truth. But it is more than that. It is also love—truth operating out of love. Man's righteousness, at best, can be only truth. But the righteousness of God is truth which operates lovingly, not severely, with forgiveness and understanding—and yet utterly consistent with truth. That is to be characteristic of the city, because it is characteristic of God.

The final words of the chapter are simply a repetition of the guarantee we saw in our previous study: the heavens and the earth, the sun and the moon, shall not pass away until God fulfills his Word. It is absolutely guaranteed. It is as true and sure as the sun's rising tomorrow morning that as you come to the Lord and trust in him and walk by faith, all the personal dilemmas of your life, and all those of the world in general, shall find their solution at the hand of the God of righteousness. He will establish what he has promised.

12

What Does God Require?

More and more in this country we are being faced with the question: What does God require, that a nation might live? What are the qualities he looks for, that permit a nation to survive in the world today? There is a remarkable answer for us in the section we come to now. Chapters 34 through 39 of Jeremiah are a series of historical flashbacks. That is, they do not come in any chronological order, but the prophet is looking back over his ministry, gathering up certain incidents which have not been reported to us before. They constitute a revelation of what God requires of a nation, and we will see dramatized in each chapter the failure of Judah to meet a requirement of God relative to the national life.

Chapter 34 goes back to the time of the second invasion of Nebuchadnezzar, after Jehoiachin (otherwise known as Coniah) had been taken captive to Babylon, and Zedekiah, the last king of Judah, was made a vassal king under Nebuchadnezzar. The Chaldean (Babylonian) army is approaching the city of Jerusalem once again, and Jeremiah is sent to the king with a message—yet another prediction of defeat at the hands of Babylon. Apparently

Zedekiah was frightened at the approach of the Babylonian army, so he began seeking ways to placate God, so
that God would feel more kindly toward him and perhaps
spare him.

I have already commented on this common phenomenon. When trouble strikes, people will often start going
to church for the first time in years, thinking that is what
God wants. Or they will start tithing, or paying their
debts, or doing something else they hope will somehow
make God feel a little more favorable toward them, as this
king sought to do. He issued a royal edict that all the
household slaves of Judah should be released from bondage.

If you look back in the fifteenth chapter of Deuteronomy, you find that the Law required that slaves—Jewish
people who had hired themselves out as servants and
slaves—were to work but six years and the seventh year
were to be freed. No Jew could be in servitude more than
six years. They could resume the contract if they wished,
but they could also choose freedom. No Jew could hold a
brother as a permanent slave.

Blasphemy

Over the years this law had fallen into disuse, and the
people had gotten used to having permanent slaves in
their households. The king evidently felt this upset God,
so he issued the edict that the slaves be released. In chapter 37, which was written at the same time, we learn that
Egypt sent an army up against Jerusalem to meet the
Babylonian army. When the Chaldeans heard that Pharaoh of Egypt was coming up against them, they left the
siege of Jerusalem and went out to meet the Egyptians.
And when king Zedekiah saw that the Babylonian army

had withdrawn, he immediately rescinded his orders to release the slaves. So God sent Jeremiah to him with a new message, which is recorded in chapter 34:

> "You recently repented and did what was right in my eyes by proclaiming liberty, each to his neighbor, and you made a covenant before me in the house which is called by my name; but then you turned around and profaned my name when each of you took back his male and female slaves, whom you had set free according to their desire, and you brought them into subjection to be your slaves. Therefore, thus says the Lord: You have not obeyed me by proclaiming liberty, every one to his brother and to his neighbor; behold, I proclaim to you liberty to the sword, to pestilence, and to famine, says the Lord. I will make you a horror to all the kingdoms of the earth" (Jer. 34:15-17).

The remarkable phrase in this passage is, "you profaned my name." This was a serious charge to any Jew. They had been brought up to revere and respect the name of God. The scribes did not even dare to write the name of God without taking a bath and changing their clothes. And they never pronounced it. The four Hebrew letters used for the name of God they called "The Ineffable Tetragrammaton"—the unpronounceable or unspeakable four letters. They never spoke the name of God. Yet God's charge against this king is, "You have profaned my name." The Hebrew word translated profane means "wound," "pierce," or "deface." God's charge is, "You have defaced me." How did Zedekiah do it? By failing to respect the human rights of slaves. It is an act of blasphemy against God to treat another person as somewhat less than a person. That is what God holds a nation to account for.

As we think of our own national history, we can see what a heavy charge must be leveled against us. How have we treated the American Indians, the original inhabitants of this land, or the Africans we brought forcibly into our midst, or the Chinese and Japanese, the Mexicans, the Puerto Ricans, and other nationalities that have come among us? We have despised them, treated them as less than human. The God of the nations says, "That is a profanation of my name. You have profaned my name when you have done a thing like that." It is always healthy for me to remember that God's view of my spirituality, his judgment of whether I am a spiritual-minded person or not, is based not upon how I treat my friends and those I like, but how I treat the waiter at the table, or the clerk in the store, or the yardman, or the newspaper boy. This is the mark of spirituality. In other words, God requires of a people that they respect the rights of all humanity. And when there is a violation of that, God takes it to account. That is the lesson of chapter 34.

In chapter 35 another matter is brought before us. Here we have the story of the Rechabites, a tribe of people who were somewhat related to Israel by marriage. These were descendants of the Kenites, the tribe of Jethro, the father-in-law of Moses. Some three hundred years before Jeremiah's time, one of their number, Rechab, was an associate of Jehu, king of Israel, at the time of Elisha. Rechab's son was Jonadab, and this account tells us that Jonadab grew tired of life in the city and longed for a simpler way of life. Many of us feel that way, wishing there were some way we could get out of the rat race and get back to nature. Jonadab evidently felt so strongly about it that he commanded his sons to drink no wine, to build no houses, and to have no vineyard or field or seed.

They were to live in tents as nomads all their lives. The sons heeded their father's commands and for almost three hundred years the tribe had traditionally followed these admonitions. When Nebuchadnezzar came up against Judah, the Rechabites took refuge in the city of Jerusalem, and Jeremiah now is sent to them by God.

The Power of Tradition

The chapter opens with God's command to Jeremiah to go to the Rechabites, bring them into the temple, and offer them wine to drink. When Jeremiah offered them wine they refused to drink it, as God knew they would. Now, this has nothing to do with the question of whether or not one should drink wine. It is clear that God never tempts anyone to evil. These Rechabites were commended not because they did not drink wine, but because they were faithful to the command of their father. Then God sent Jeremiah to the nation of Judah with these words, beginning with verse 12:

> Then the word of the Lord came to Jeremiah: "Thus says the Lord of hosts, the God of Israel: Go and say to the men of Judah and the inhabitants of Jerusalem, Will you not receive instruction and listen to my words? says the Lord. The command which Jonadab the son of Rechab gave to his sons, to drink no wine, has been kept; and they drink none to this day, for they have obeyed their father's command. I have spoken to you persistently, but you have not listened to me. I have sent to you all my servants the prophets, sending them persistently, saying, 'Turn now every one of you from his evil way, and amend your doings, and do not go after other gods to serve them, and then you shall dwell in the land which I gave to

you and your fathers.' But you did not incline
your ear to listen to me. The sons of Jonadab the
son of Rechab have kept the command which their
father gave them, but this people has not obeyed
me" (Jer. 35:12–16).

It would be very easy to misread this passage—as though
God were simply commending these Rechabites for their
fidelity to their father's wishes. He does do that. In fact,
later on in the passage he promises them that they "shall
never lack a man to stand before" him. (I wonder if this
does not suggest that it is possible to trace the origin of
Gypsies back to these Rechabites, because they live exactly this way today.) But the real point of the passage
is not so much that the Rechabites were commended for
keeping their father's command, but rather that Judah
is reproved because the nation would not obey God. In
other words, the power of tradition has greater force with
men than the revelation of the living God. The Rechabites
were under the grip of their father's whim, and were
obedient to his request three hundred years after he had
made it. "But," God says, "I who am among you as a
living God, speaking to you through the prophets persistently, trying to correct the evils in the life of this nation, am paid no attention whatsoever." The evil reflected
here is the power of tradition, holding men's minds in its
ironclad grip, rather than allowing them to respond to the
revelation of a living God.

The dead hand of the past is with us yet today in many,
many ways, still holding us in that grip. On the national
level it is apparent in that politicians are afraid to move
unless a precedent has been established. Have you noticed
that? They look about for a precedent, and if there has
been none, they lack the courage to stand for right against

wrong. So they seek ways to compromise and to make it appear they are doing the right thing when they are not. This is because man loves tradition above anything else.

The church is gripped by it as well. As I have traveled about the country I have seen hundreds of churches which are so held in the iron grip of the past that they feel unable to obey God in what he is saying to them in the present hour. The power of tradition sits as a great blight upon Christian people across this land. In a cartoon I saw recently portraying the dead church, were these words—the seven last words of the church written across its tombstone: "Nothing like this has ever happened before." That is the power of man's tradition. Thomas Dixon once said,

> Tradition was the most constant, the most persistent, the most dogged, the most utterly devilish opposition the Master encountered. It openly attacked Him on every hand, and silently repulsed His teaching. Even the Samaritan woman He finds armed with the ancestral bludgeon, "Art thou greater than our father Jacob? *Our* fathers worshipped in *this* mountain." Without departure from customs there could have been no Christian church. The great soul-winners of the past had to shake off the shackles of overconservatism in methods—witness Melanchthon, Wesley, Edwards, Finney. The church grows by iconoclasm. Its first work is to set aside false gods.

This chapter of Jeremiah reveals that God requires of a nation, or of a church, a continual review of the methods of the past in the flashing light of the revelation of God today. If we are not going back over and over, reviewing what has been done in the past, and asking ourselves, "Is this in line with what we understand *now* to be the truth, to be reality as God has revealed it?" we are certain to sink more and more into the ooze and mire of tradition, to be lost in its swamps.

In chapter 36 there is another revelation of what God requires of a nation. Here we have the story of how this Book of Jeremiah came to be written. It takes us back to the fourth year of Jehoiakim the son of Josiah, king of Judah, at about the midpoint of Jeremiah's ministry. God commanded the prophet to write down in a book all the things he had been saying. Up to this point he had been giving oral messages to the people, but now God commanded him to write them down in a book. So he called his secretary Baruch, and dictated the messages to him. Then, since he was a prisoner and unable to go himself, he sent Baruch to read them in the temple.

Baruch waited until all the people from the cities around Jerusalem had come to the temple on a day of fasting, and read to them the words God had given Jeremiah for them. Jeremiah and Baruch hoped the people would repent and turn, and then God would restore the nation. One of the princes heard Baruch reading this book, and told the other princes what he had heard. They gathered together and sent for Baruch to read it again to them. The account says that when they heard it, they trembled in fear because of what God had said, and said to each other, "We must report this to the king." We take up the account at verse 20:

> So they went into the court to the king, having put the scroll in the chamber of Elishama the secretary; and they reported all the words to the king [Jehoiakim]. Then the king sent Jehudi to get the scroll, and he took it from the chamber of Elishama

the secretary; and Jehudi read it to the king and all the princes who stood beside the king. It was the ninth month [December], and the king was sitting in the winter house and there was a fire burning in the brazier before him. As Jehudi read three or four columns, the king would cut them off with a penknife and throw them into the fire in the brazier, until the entire scroll was consumed in the fire that was in the brazier. [Here was the first destructive critic of the Scriptures!] Yet neither the king, nor any of his servants who heard all these words, was afraid, nor did they rend their garments. Even when Elnathan and Delaiah and Gemariah urged the king not to burn the scroll, he would not listen to them. And the king commanded Jerahmeel the king's son and Saraiah the son of Azri-el and Shelemiah the son of Abdeel to seize Baruch the secretary and Jeremiah the prophet, but the Lord hid them (Jer. 36:20–26).

Because of this contemptuous act of defiance, in which king Jehoiakim brazenly cut the scroll to pieces and threw it into the fire as it was read, he was condemned. Later in this chapter Jeremiah is sent with the message that he was condemned to destruction and to humiliation. His body would be thrown out to the heat of the day and the cold of the night, to be eaten by dogs. Jeremiah was told to write the words again, verse 32:

Then Jeremiah took another scroll and gave it to Baruch the scribe, the son of Neriah, who wrote on it at the dictation of Jeremiah all the words of the scroll which Jehoiakim king of Judah had burned in the fire; and many similar words were added to them.

Instead of eliminating the Scripture, the king had only added to it. That is the way God works. And this scroll is now the present Book of Jeremiah.

The Fear of God

The point this passage makes is that judgment came against this king not simply because he acted foolishly in burning the Scriptures but because of the condition of heart which that action revealed. This is given to us in one flaming sentence in verse 24: "Yet neither the king, nor any of his servants who heard all these words, was afraid, nor did they rend their garments." These men had lost the fear of God. And when a nation or a people or an individual loses the fear of God, they are on their way to destruction. For the fear of God is based upon the sovereign power which he exercises in life. These men were shown to be stupid and senseless men who had lost their sense of reality entirely, because they had lost the fear of God.

There is one great fact everywhere revealed—in Scripture, in history, and even in nature—which has been called "the law of retribution." That is, there is an inevitable consequence for doing wrong, and there is no way to escape it. Even an atheist, who does not believe in God at all, must admit that when he examines the laws of nature he is faced with the conclusion that you either obey the laws of nature and live, or disobey them and die, one or the other. And man is helpless to change that. We are in the grip of forces greater than we are, and everything on every side testifies to this. That is why we learn respect for the laws of electricity. You do not fool around with 10,000 volts of electrical potential, thinking you are going to make up the laws as you go along. You had better find out what they are first, for you disobey them to your peril and death.

This is what God has implanted in every part of life. How foolish and utterly stupid is the person who seeks to ignore that fact. God requires of every nation that there be the recognition of his sovereign government of men, and the law of retribution for evil. History has testified again and again that God always accomplishes what he says he is going to do. God rules in the affairs of men. Therefore the basic, elementary knowledge of life with which everyone ought to start is the fear of God. Proverbs says, "The fear of God is the beginning of all wisdom."

In chapters 37 and 38, which we will take together since they constitute one account, we find another thing God requires of nations. In these chapters we have the story of the persecution of Jeremiah, which took place when the Babylonians had withdrawn from Jerusalem to face Pharaoh's army. God sent Jeremiah to Zedekiah to say that Nebuchadnezzar would return, that the armies of Babylon would be back again at Jerusalem. Verses 11–15 give us an incident concerning Jeremiah:

> Now when the Chaldean army had withdrawn from Jerusalem at the approach of Pharaoh's army, Jeremiah set out from Jerusalem to go to the land of Benjamin to receive his portion there among the people. When he was at the Benjamin Gate, a sentry there named Irijah the son of Shelemiah, son of Hananiah, seized Jeremiah the prophet, saying, "You are deserting to the Chaldeans." And Jeremiah said, "It is false; I am not deserting to the Chaldeans." But Irijah would not listen to him, and seized Jeremiah and brought him to the princes. And the princes were enraged at Jeremiah,

> and they beat him and imprisoned him in the
> house of Jonathan the secretary, for it had been
> made a prison (Jer. 37:11–15).

This is the account of how Jeremiah first became a prisoner. A little later, at the request of king Zedekiah, he
was permitted to be a house prisoner, and given a little
more liberty. Chapter 38 tells us how the princes became
angry, as Jeremiah continually counseled surrender to
the Babylonians. Beginning at verse 4 the account says,

> Then the princes said to the king, "Let this man be
> put to death, for he is weakening the hands of the
> soldiers who are left in this city, and the hands of
> all the people, by speaking such words to them.
> For this man is not seeking the welfare of this peo-
> ple, but their harm." King Zedekiah said, "Behold,
> he is in your hands; for the king can do nothing
> against you." So they took Jeremiah and cast him
> into the cistern of Malchiah, the king's son, which
> was in the court of the guard, letting Jeremiah
> down by ropes. And there was no water in the
> cistern, but only mire, and Jeremiah sank in the
> mire (Jer. 38:4–6).

We might well say that this was the low point in Jeremiah's career! Down in the mud and gloom of that dank,
dark cistern, with no food and no water, no adequate
clothing, he was covered over and left alone to die. As far
as he was concerned, he thought he *would* die, but God
had not forgotten his prophet. What a revelation this
incident is of how foolish we are when we think that being faithful to the ministry God has given us will guarantee that we will be delivered from all troubles. Here was
a man who was faithful to do what God had said, but
God allowed him to be put into the cistern.

Jeremiah thought it was all over for him, but God has his men in all sorts of places. In the court of the king was an Ethiopian eunuch, a black servant, whose name is given here as Ebed-melech. But Ebed-melech, in Hebrew, means "the servant of the king." So I do not think this was his name at all, but rather, a description of *what* he was: the king's servant. He was a nameless man. "Hey, you," they must have called him. And God sent "Hey you" down to deliver Jeremiah. He went before the king, verse 9, and said,

> "My lord the king, these men have done evil in all that they did to Jeremiah the prophet by casting him into the cistern; and he will die there of hunger, for there is no bread left in the city." Then the king commanded Ebed-melech, the Ethiopian, "Take three men with you from here, and lift Jeremiah the prophet out of the cistern before he dies." So Ebed-melech took the men with him and went to the house of the king, to a wardrobe of the storehouse, and took from there old rags and worn-out clothes, which he let down to Jeremiah in the cistern by ropes. Then Ebed-melech the Ethiopian said to Jeremiah, "Put the rags and clothes between your armpits and the ropes." Jeremiah did so. Then they drew Jeremiah up with ropes and lifted him out of the cistern. And Jeremiah remained in the court of the guard (Jer. 38:9–13).

What tender, loving, compassionate care this dear man manifested toward the prophet! Lest the rope injure Jeremiah as he was lifted up, he provided rags to cushion it. And Jeremiah spent the rest of his time in the court of the guard, until Jerusalem was taken.

The account goes on to say how king Zedekiah, aware

that Jeremiah indeed was a true man of God, sent for him and asked for a word from God. This weak and vacillating king nevertheless wanted to hear what the prophet had to say. Jeremiah assured him of safety if he would but surrender to the Babylonian army. But the king was afraid. Like Pilate, many centuries later, he did not have the courage of his convictions; he was too afraid of those around him. So the king sent Jeremiah back to the court of the guard.

What does this reveal about what God expects of a nation? Well, God requires that a nation listen to the authorized spokesman of God. Over and over again in Scripture you find God identifying with his people! When young Saul of Tarsus asked, "Who are you, Lord?" Jesus said, "I am Jesus whom thou art persecuting." Paul was persecuting Christians, but Jesus said, "You're persecuting me." When Jesus sent his disciples out, he told them to go into all the cities of Israel. And he said, "If they receive you they have received me." Later Jesus himself wept over the city of Jerusalem: "O Jerusalem, Jerusalem, killing the prophets and stoning those who are sent to you! How often would I have gathered your children together as a hen gathers her brood under her wings, and you would not!" God holds to account a nation that rejects the authorized voice of God in its midst.

In the opening words of chapter 39 there is a very brief account of the actual overthrow of the city:

> In the ninth year of Zedekiah king of Judah, in the tenth month, Nebuchadrezzar king of Babylon and all his army came against Jerusalem and besieged it; in the eleventh year of Zedekiah, in the fourth month, on the ninth day of the month, a

breach was made in the city. When Jerusalem was taken, all the princes of the king of Babylon came and sat in the middle gate: . . . [their names are then listed]. When Zedekiah king of Judah and all the soldiers saw them, they fled, going out of the city at night by way of the king's garden through the gate between the two walls; and they went toward the Arabah. But the army of the Chaldeans pursued them, and overtook Zedekiah in the plains of Jericho; and when they had taken him, they brought him up to Nebuchadrezzar king of Babylon, at Riblah, in the land of Hamath; and he passed sentence upon him. The king of Babylon slew the sons of Zedekiah at Riblah before his eyes; and the king of Babylon slew all the nobles of Judah. He put out the eyes of Zedekiah, and bound him in fetters to take him to Babylon. The Chaldeans burned the king's house and the house of the people, and broke down the walls of Jerusalem (Jer. 39:1–8).

In the further historic detail given in the last chapter of Jeremiah, we are told that they burned the temple of God as well. The long-delayed hour of judgment came at last. The city was taken. The women were ravished. The temple was burned. The king's eyes were put out. As you read this account you can see a certain poetic justice which is always characteristic of the judgments of God. The city that refused God, God refused. He granted them their own desire, in other words. The temple that burned incense to idols was itself burned. The king who would not see had his eyes put out. The people who held their slaves captive were themselves led captive by the Babylonians. This is always the way God works. His judgment is to give you exactly what you are asking for, to let you finally have your way—but to the fullest extent, beyond anything you would desire.

Judgment Will Come

So the last requirement of God that we can see in this account is that a nation must never forget that, ultimately, the judgment of God will come. "The mills of God grind slow, but they grind exceeding small." Sooner or later judgment will fall. God himself said, in Ezekiel, "I will overturn, overturn, overturn, till he shall come whose right it is to reign." No nation has the right to continue to exist as a nation when it continually violates these requirements of God's justice. Therefore the hand of doom rests upon any nation that deliberately refuses to hear and heed the will of God. Ultimately, judgment will come. No political manipulation will avert it. No partial compromise will delay, no defiance will evade what God has said. It will come at last—some eleventh year, ninth month, and fourth day, when a breach is made in the walls of the city, and judgment and destruction can no longer be averted.

I want to gather up four things from this account which are of significance to us today. We find here four ways by which individuals and nations seek to turn aside the will of God, and all are present in our nation today. First, a people can ignore and refuse to listen to God, and give themselves over to things that help to forget, living a life of debauchery and revelry, refusing to hear and heed the Word of God. That is happening in America, as you well know. Second, a people can persecute the prophets of God, and hinder the message of God. Perhaps that is more visible in the Communist world today than it is here, but in America an increasingly callous attitude is developing against the preaching of the Word of God. Third, a people can seek to circumvent the catastrophe which is coming by political maneuverings and manipulations. That is the whole story of Watergate—an attempt to escape the ultimate judgment of moral wrong by cover-ups and pretenses and bribery. But it cannot work. And finally, a people can compromise in outward ways, but fall short of real submission to God. That is when a people become outwardly religious—learn the "God-words" and practice civil religion—but their hearts remain unchanged.

There is only one attitude that will avert the coming judgment of God: repentance, deep humiliation before God, acknowledgment of guilt, a willingness to recognize that we have lost our right to exist as a nation, and a cry to God that he will heal us and change us and forgive us and heal this land. When that occurs, God himself assumes responsibility to recover the nation. Despite all the damage which has been done, he will restore the years that the locusts have eaten, and the nation will come again to power and righteousness and leadership in the affairs of the world. But if a nation ignores God, it goes down into the dust of history, as hundreds of kingdoms and nations before us have perished. "Lord of hosts, be with us yet, lest we forget, lest we forget."

13

Back to Egypt

In our last study we saw Jeremiah's description of the fall of Jerusalem to the armies of Babylon, an event which had hovered on the horizon of his ministry throughout his life. God had delayed that judgment while Jeremiah ministered to this people, seeking to turn them about, seeking to prevent, if he could, the death of this nation. God's patience is evident in this book, because it was forty years before the judgment he had announced finally came.

But now Jerusalem has fallen, and in chapters 40 through 45 we have the account of what happened in the nation after the destruction of Jerusalem. One would think the overthrow of the city would be enough to turn the hearts of the people back to God. But not so. This people had not yet reached bottom. In our study we will see how they are led by the deceitfulness of the flesh into that place of utter and insolent rebellion against God which marked the very nadir of their downfall.

This is a very instructive lesson for all of us. Remember that the New Testament tells us that all these stories in the Old Testament are recorded for *our* instruction, in order that we might learn something about ourselves.

There is a double meaning in these Old Testament stories. Not only are they historical events, but also, we will learn something more about the nature and functioning of that strange tendency toward evil within each of us called in the Bible "the flesh"—the old life, the inherent Adamic nature. One of the most important things we can learn as Christians is how to recognize the flesh. Remember the verse back in the seventeenth chapter of Jeremiah which probably is the most often-quoted in this book:

> The heart is deceitful above all things,
>   and desperately corrupt;
>   who can understand it? (Jer. 17:9)

These chapters are a great commentary on that verse, on the deceitfulness of the heart—how it works to deceive us and mislead us. This account is a story of the flesh at work. And it will drive us to an awareness that only by trust in the living God can we ever hope to overcome the deceitfulness of the flesh. As we go through it I want simply to point out the various forms the flesh takes and the ways in which it operates to deceive us. We will find them reflected in our own natures.

In chapter 40 we have the account of Jeremiah's experience after the capture of Jerusalem. He is freed by Nebuzardan, the captain of the guard under Nebuchadnezzar, and given his choice as to where to live. He can go to Babylon, and there be treated with honor and respect, or he can stay in the land. Jeremiah chooses to stay in the land and to associate himself with Gedaliah, the governor appointed by the king of Babylon to rule over this nation: "Then Jeremiah went to Gedaliah the son of Ahikam, at Mizpah, and dwelt with him among the people who were left in the land" (Jer. 40:6). Then the account tells us there were still unsubdued Judean warriors who gathered themselves into roving guerrilla bands under various captains—Ishmael, Johanan, Seraiah, and Jezaniah. They came to Gedaliah at Mizpah, who told them that if they would but submit to the government of Babylon, God would bless them and give them peace in the land. But they were rebellious, refused to do this, and continued their guerrilla warfare against Babylon. In verses 13 through 16 we have an incident that is instructive to us:

> Now Johanan the son of Kareah and all the leaders of the forces in the open country came to Gedaliah at Mizpah and said to him, "Do you know that Baalis the king of the Ammonites has sent Ishmael the son of Nethaniah to take your life?" But Gedaliah the son of Ahikam would not believe them. Then Johanan the son of Kareah spoke secretly to Gedaliah at Mizpah, "Let me go and slay Ishmael the son of Nethaniah, and no one will know it. Why should he take your life, so that all the Jews who are gathered about you would be scattered, and the remnant of Judah would perish?" But Gedaliah the son of Ahikam said to Johanan the son of Kareah, "You shall not do this thing, for you are speaking falsely of Ishmael."

One of the most subtle manifestations of the old nature within us is its tendency to be trustful of everybody, without discrimination. The Scriptures make clear that it is wrong for us always to be suspicious of people. If you are the kind of person who never trusts anybody, who is always defensive and suspicious, this is a serious weakness that will get you in a great deal of trouble. But on the other hand, to be naïve and ingenuous, to believe everyone who comes along, is also a weakness.

Pairs of Opposites

As we have seen many times in studying the Scriptures, the devil sends error into the world in pairs of opposites—as far apart from each other as is possible to get—and yet each is an aspect of the same error. Satan's trick is to try to get you to flee from one aspect so that you will fall into the other. He does this all the time. The course of the Christian must be a narrow, fence-balancing walk right between the extremes. It is difficult to maintain, except as we walk with God. Only he has the wisdom to maintain our balance.

Here we find a man who is naïve, who believes everyone, who has an undiscerning trust, and he will not believe this threat against his life. Yet the man who tries to warn him also has a flaw in his character. His way of correcting this situation is to take a secret vengeance upon Ishmael. If Gedaliah had been aware of the meaning of names, he would have been tipped off by the name "Ishmael." Ishmael was the name of the brother of Isaac. The New Testament calls him a picture of the man of the flesh, the man who cannot be trusted. All the men in Scripture who bear this name are of this character. This Ishmael has been bribed by the king of the Ammonites to take the life of Gedaliah. But Gedaliah is trusting, and never tests the spirits, as God tells us to do, to see which is of God and which is not. And so he refuses to believe this of Ishmael, and it costs him his life, as we will see.

Johanan wants to take vengeance by quietly going to Ishmael and murdering him in secret. This again is a manifestation of the flesh, that feeling that somehow, without people finding out, we can get by with doing the wrong thing for the right motive. The terrible, deadly danger of the flesh that deceives us is to make us think a thing is right when it really is wrong.

This man wanted to take a secret vengeance. I have some personal experience of that kind of attitude. Every now and then I get letters which just take me apart, blister me, list all my faults—and, of course, the discouraging thing about it is that the writers are often right! But there are obvious areas of misunderstanding as well, to which I would like to respond with a note of explanation. But when I come to the end of such a letter, there is no signature—it is merely another anonymous note. I have learned to treat these with disdain, because an anonymous note is a way of striking at somebody secretly without letting the person know who you are, without having enough of the courage of your convictions to sign what you write.

Now in chapter 41 we have the outcome of Gedaliah's misplaced trust:

> In the seventh month, Ishmael the son of Nethaniah, son of Elishama, of the royal family, one of the chief officers of the king, came with ten men to Gedaliah the son of Ahikam, at Mizpah. As they ate bread together there at Mizpah, Ishmael the son of Nethaniah and the ten men with him rose up and struck down Gedaliah the son of Ahikam, son of Shaphan, with the sword, and killed him, whom the king of Babylon had appointed governor in the land. Ishmael also slew all the Jews who were with Gedaliah at Mizpah, and the Chaldean soldiers who happened to be there (Jer. 41:1–3).

This is a bloody account, an account of treachery and jealousy. Ishmael was of the royal family, one of the chief officers of the king. Perhaps that accounts for his jealousy of the man who, though of humble origin, had been appointed governor of the land. So in a scene of apparent harmony, while they were eating bread together, he rises and smites him with the sword and kills him—and not only Gedaliah but all the others who were with him in the palace of Mizpah. This picture of treachery and murder reveals what lies hidden in our own hearts. Any time we get angry and upset, we feel this same kind of murderous rage within. At that moment, given the opportunity, if we felt that nothing bad would result, we would probably take somebody's life. Hating a brother is murder, the Scriptures say, and hate is a characteristic of the flesh we live with. When Cain was disappointed that God had rejected his offering, God warned him: "Sin is crouching at the door, like a lion ready to spring on you and drive you into something that is worse." Cain did not heed that warning, and went on to murder his brother. I remember a tragic instance many years ago of a pastor's son who grew up to be a criminal, and finally, coming home one day in a fit of murderous rage, he slew his own mother. This is possible for any of us, given the right circumstance, because this is the nature of the flesh within us.

Unreasoning Fear

As we read on, the situation gets worse. This man Ishmael trapped eighty men who arrived in Mizpah bringing their offerings. He slew them and filled a cistern with their bodies. Then he took captive the rest of the inhabitants of Mizpah, including Jeremiah, intending to deliver them to the Ammonites. But the forces led by Johanan the son of Kareah rescued them. We pick up the account at verse 16:

> Then Johanan the son of Kareah and all the leaders of the forces with him took all the rest of the people whom Ishmael the son of Nethaniah had carried away captive from Mizpah after he had slain Gedaliah the son of Ahikam—soldiers, women, children, and eunuchs, whom Johanan brought back from Gibeon. And they went and stayed at Geruth Chimham near Bethlehem, intending to go to Egypt because of the Chaldeans; for they were afraid of them, because Ishmael the son of Nethaniah had slain Gedaliah the son of Ahikam, whom the king of Babylon had made governor over the land (Jer. 41:16–18).

That is strange! These innocent people were fleeing from the Babylonians. Yet it was the Babylonians who had appointed Gedaliah governor over the land, and they would have avenged his death. These men, who were not involved in this murder, had no reason to fear the Babylonians. But they fled from them nevertheless. This is a further revelation of what the evil heart within us does; it makes us afraid of that which we need not fear. Unreasonable fear comes to us, and we begin to fear all kinds of things. Proverbs says, "The wicked flee when no man pursues." This is true. Here are men whose consciences are not yet fully right before God. And so, though they have not been involved in these murders, nevertheless they flee, and all the people with them, down to Egypt where they had no business going.

Our hearts are often given over to this kind of unjustified fear. My mind goes back to the days when I was in the navy in Hawaii. We had an Italian barber at the naval base whom we all enjoyed taking to the movies because he got so involved emotionally in the story that he would get carried away and do all kinds of strange things. We enjoyed watching him instead of the movie! If a villain started to attack some innocent person, he would jump up and shake his fist, and everybody in the house would start laughing at him. On one occasion something frightening was happening on the screen, and he suddenly leaped from his seat and ran out of the theater, crying out in fear. This is what I thought of when I read this account—running from shadows on a screen. Have you ever done that? When the heart is not right, everything looks threatening, and anxieties grip you. You are afraid, fearful of anything, everything, troubled all the time by a foreboding sense of impending disaster. That is the work of the flesh within us.

In chapter 42 we read on:

> Then all the commanders of the forces, and Johanan the son of Kareah and Azariah the son of Hoshaiah, and all the people from the least to the greatest, came near and said to Jeremiah the prophet, "Let our supplication come before you, and pray to the Lord your God for us, for all this remnant (for we are left but a few of many, as your eyes see us), that the Lord your God may show us the way we should go, and the thing that we should do." Jeremiah the prophet said to them, "I have heard you; behold, I will pray to the Lord your God according to your request, and whatever the Lord answers you I will tell you; I will keep nothing back from you." Then they said to Jeremiah, "May the Lord be a true and faithful witness against us if we do not act according to all the

word with which the Lord your God sends you to
us. Whether it is good or evil, we will obey the
voice of the Lord our God to whom we are sending
you, that it may be well with us when we obey the
voice of the Lord our God" (Jer. 42:1–6).

Well, it looks as if they are straightening out, does it not?
At last they are doing the right thing, coming to Jeremiah
and saying, "Is it right to go to Egypt?" Now, they knew
it was not, because the Scriptures had always said that
Israel was never to go back to Egypt—never. "Woe unto
them that trust in Egypt," Isaiah said. And yet here they
are on their way. So they come, as so many Christians do,
wanting to find a scriptural way to disobey God. They
tell Jeremiah the prophet, "You go and ask God whether
it's right for us to do this or not. And whatever he tells
you, we'll do it."

Right Words, Wrong Hearts

Notice a revealing detail in their phraseology. In verses
2 and 3 they say, "Let our supplication come before you,
and pray to the Lord *your* God for us . . . that the Lord
your God may show us the way we should go . . ."
There is a sense of distance from God already. But Jeremiah will have nothing of this. He says, "I have heard
you; behold, I will pray to the Lord *your* God according
to your request, and whatever the Lord answers *you* I
will tell you . . ." He refuses to be a middleman, a
mediator, but insists that they deal directly with God
himself. And he goes to the Lord with this request of
theirs.

So their words sound good, but their hearts are wrong,
as subsequent events prove. They knew this was wrong,
and yet they wanted somehow to use God to justify their

actions, so they clothe them with these pious words. That again is a manifestation of the flesh. The flesh can be extremely religious. It loves to sing in the choir, to usher, to preach messages, and do all kinds of other religious things—as long as it can have an evil heart of unbelief. That is what these people had.

I have long ago learned that when people start talking to me of "the good Lord," it is time to get suspicious. That phrase is usually used by the world, and often by carnal Christians, when they want to talk about God. They call him "the good Lord." Now, this is not true of everyone who uses the phrase, and I do not want to stigmatize anyone who does. But I get suspicious when I hear it because I know that those who know God usually do not call him "the good Lord," but just "the Lord."

Here is the reply they get, verse 7:

> At the end of ten days the word of the Lord came to Jeremiah. Then he summoned Johanan the son of Kareah and all the commanders of the forces who were with him, and all the people from the least to the greatest [God made these people wait in the waiting room for ten days, cooling their heels, before he gave Jeremiah the answer], and said to them, "Thus says the Lord, the God of Israel, to whom you sent me to present your supplication before him: If you will remain in this land, then I will build you up and not pull you down; I will plant you, and not pluck you up; for I repent of the evil which I did to you. Do not fear the king of Babylon, of whom you are afraid; do not fear him, says the Lord, for I am with you, to save you and to deliver you from his hand. I will grant you mercy, that he may have mercy on you

and let you remain in your own land. [They had nothing to fear if they would obey God.] But if you say, 'We will not remain in this land,' disobeying the voice of the Lord your God and saying, 'No. we will go to the land of Egypt, where we shall not see war, or hear the sound of the trumpet, or be hungry for bread, and we will dwell there,' then hear the word of the Lord, O remnant of Judah. . . . All the men who set their faces to go to Egypt to live there shall die by the sword, by famine, and by pestilence" (Jer. 42:7–15, 17).

Do you see how thoroughly God knew their hearts? He knew what they were saying in their inner hearts: "Ah, down in Egypt we'll have no trouble. If we go to Egypt, everything's going to be fine. There'll be no famine in Egypt, no war in Egypt, no draft, no drills. Everything will be fine in Egypt." This is another characteristic of the flesh. It not only arouses within us these unreasoning fears, but it also leads us to trust in baseless hopes, to imagine that "everything's going to be all right" in some place other than that of God's choosing.

Is it not amazing how we succumb to the temptation to run? What were they running down to Egypt to escape? The sword, famine, pestilence. What did God say they would find when they got to Egypt? The sword, famine, pestilence. You see, you cannot run away from God. You bring your troubles with you. You cannot run to some other place and escape. A change of scenery is not going to relieve you, because the problem is within. "The heart is deceitful above all things, and desperately corrupt; who can understand it?" The chapter goes on to affirm how God, with a certainty, will bring this judgment on them. Chapter 43 continues the account:

When Jeremiah finished speaking to all the people all these words of the Lord their God, with
which the Lord their God had sent him to them,
Azariah the son of Hoshaiah and Johanan the son
of Kareah and all the insolent men said to Jeremiah. "You are telling a lie. The Lord our God did
not send you to say, 'Do not go to Egypt to live
there'; but Baruch the son of Neriah has sent you
against us, to deliver us into the hand of the Chaldeans, that they may kill us or take us into exile
in Babylon." So Johanan the son of Kareah and all
the commanders of the forces and all the people
did not obey the voice of the Lord, to remain in the
land of Judah (Jer. 43:1–4).

Isn't it strange? To this prophet's face, after forty years
or more of his ministry of highest integrity, they dared
to say, "You are telling a lie. God didn't send you." They
justified it by blaming someone else. "Baruch did it."
Have you ever done that? Have you ever blamed someone
else for your own problem, put the blame on somebody
else who is involved, but who is not really the cause? The
flesh loves to transfer blame. And blaming another is
almost always the mark of the flesh in action, deceiving
you, leading you on into worse things than you have ever
known before.

So the people come down to Egypt despite the word of
God. This people, who had been delivered from Egypt
900 years before by the power of God, is now back in
Egypt again, back in the land of bondage, the land of
peril.

Rocks of Witness

Then the word of the Lord came to Jeremiah down in
Egypt, at Tahpanhes. The word of God is never bound.

The people of God may be bound, but not the word of God. The word comes to Jeremiah and tells him again to perform one of those strange, graphic illustrations of truth. He is to take large stones and hide them in the mortar of the pavement at the entrance to Pharaoh's house in Tahpanhes, as a testimony to the fact that Nebuchadnezzar the king of Babylon would come down to Egypt and spread his royal canopy above these stones. The thing they were trying to escape in Judah, they would find in Egypt. The king of Babylon would be there. Some years ago Sir Flinders Petrie, the English Egyptologist, digging in the very location of the ancient city of Tahpanhes, found a pavement with large stones embedded in it. Jeremiah's stones are still there, and they were a testimony to this people that God would confirm his word to them. They would find in Egypt what they were fleeing from.

In chapter 44 we have the sequel. The people spread through the land of Egypt rather rapidly. Jeremiah calls them all together after they have been there a few months and announces to them that they are still doing the same things that brought judgment on them in Judah. The very things God objected to they are now resuming in Egypt. The women were the leaders in this, offering incense to the queen of heaven, that is, the moon goddess, and giving themselves in idolatrous ways to the other Egyptian gods around them as well. That is what God judged Judah for, as Jeremiah reminds them. He tells them God will judge them here in this land too. Here is the reaction of the people, beginning at verse 15:

> Then all the men who knew that their wives had offered incense to other gods, and all the women who stood by, a great assembly, all the people who dwelt in Pathros in the land of Egypt,

> answered Jeremiah: "As for the word which you
> have spoken to us in the name of the Lord, we will
> not listen to you. But we will do everything that
> we have vowed, burn incense to the queen of
> heaven and pour out libations to her, as we did,
> both we and our fathers, our kings and our princes,
> in the cities of Judah and in the streets of Jeru-
> salem . . ."

This was an act of open defiance, of rebellious insolence,
in which they said to Jeremiah, "We don't care what you
say or what God says. We're going to do what we want."
So their defiance comes at last into the open. They justified it on these grounds:

> ". . . for then [i.e., back in Judah] we had plenty
> of food, and prospered, and saw no evil. But since
> we left off burning incense to the queen of heaven
> and pouring out libations to her, we have lacked
> everything and have been consumed by the sword
> and by famine" (Jer. 44:15–18).

Isn't it strange how quickly the mind of the flesh can
forget? Because they did have trouble in Judah—plenty
of it. And the extent to which they had less trouble and
more prosperity there was due not to their actions but to
the grace of God, withholding judgment. But they could
not see that. Because things were a little better in Judah
they said, "Our trouble now is that we have offended the
queen of heaven." So they go back to their idolatry and
insolently refuse to obey.

God's Name Removed

Here is the judgment that falls on them. It marks the
deepest level of decay of this nation:

"Therefore hear the word of the Lord, all you of
Judah who dwell in the land of Egypt: Behold, I
have sworn by my great name, says the Lord, that
my name shall no more be invoked by the mouth
of any man of Judah in all the land of Egypt,
saying, 'As the Lord God lives.' Behold, I am
watching over them for evil and not for good; all
the men of Judah who are in the land of Egypt
shall be consumed by the sword and by famine,
until there is an end of them. And those who escape
the sword shall return from the land of Egypt to
the land of Judah, few in number; and all the
remnant of Judah, who came to the land of Egypt
to live, shall know whose word will stand, mine
or theirs" (Jer. 44:26–28).

God takes up the challenge they throw down to him, and
he says that the judgment which falls upon them is that
his name is removed from them. I do not know exactly
what that meant in terms of practice in the life of this
people, though I am sure it meant something very real.
Very likely it was that they lost all sense of the existence
of God. They lost the sense of God's presence in the
world.

We live in a day when all around us people have lost
the sense of the existence of God, and the result is terrible
to watch. People have a sense of cosmic loneliness. They
feel that man is abandoned, alone in the universe, and
that all the tremendously complex problems of the world
are his alone to solve. And many recognize that man has
no ability to solve them. The result is a terrible, sinking
despair that grips the heart. We see it all around us today. That is probably what happened in Egypt—that
sense of despair as these people lost the sense of their
refuge in the name of God. It is an advantage to the man

or woman who is disobeying God to realize that God is still there—someone to go back to. But when you lose that sense, there is nothing left but loneliness and despair.

Chapter 45, which is the briefest chapter of the book—only five verses—gives us the final picture of the flesh in action. This chapter comes from the time when Jeremiah sent Baruch down to the temple to read the words he had dictated, as we saw earlier. Chronologically it should follow chapter 36. But Jeremiah has placed it right here because it gathers up the tendency of the heart which is behind all these manifestations of the flesh.

> The word that Jeremiah the prophet spoke to Baruch the son of Neriah, when he wrote these words in a book at the dictation of Jeremiah, in the fourth year of Jehoiakim the son of Josiah, king of Judah: "Thus says the Lord, the God of Israel, to you, O Baruch: You said, 'Woe is me! for the Lord has added sorrow to my pain; I am weary with my groaning, and I find no rest' " (Jer. 45:1–3).

Beruch had been sent down to the temple to read the words of the Lord, and this passage is telling us what he evidently felt in his own heart. He expected that his reading would have a tremendous impact upon the people, and that he himself would be exalted before them as the spokesman of God, and would be lifted up in their eyes. But it did not work that way. Instead, they rejected the words and they rejected Baruch. He went home feeling terrible about it, feeling that his whole ministry was useless. And he cried out to God this way: "Woe is me! for the Lord has added sorrow to my pain; I am weary with my groaning, and I find no rest." So God sent Jeremiah to him with this message:

"Thus shall you say to him, Thus says the Lord:
Behold, what I have built I am breaking down,
and what I have planted I am plucking up—that
is, the whole land. And do you seek great things
for yourself? Seek them not; for, behold, I am
bringing evil upon all flesh, says the Lord; but I
will give you your life as a prize of war in all places
to which you may go" (Jer. 45:4–5).

What is the root of all our troubles with the flesh? It is
seeking great things for ourselves. That is behind the
naïveté, the secret vengeance, the treachery and murder,
the unjustified fear, the pious deceit, the baseless hopes,
the misdirected blame, the insolent rebellion—all of these
arise out of a heart which longs to have glory that belongs
to God. That is the basic problem, is it not?

As we look at this we say to ourselves, "Who is suffi-
cient for these things? How can we lick this terrible
enemy within?" The only answer, of course, is the cross
and the resurrection of Jesus. This is all that has ever
been able to deal with the flesh in man's life: the cross
which puts it to death; the resurrection which provides
another life in its place. That is the glory of the gospel.

Near Watsonville, California, there is a creek that has
a strange name: Salsipuedes Creek. "Sal si puedes" is
Spanish for "Get out of it if you can." The creek is lined
with quicksand, and the story is that many years ago, in
the early days of California, a Mexican laborer fell into
the quicksand. A Spaniard, riding by on a horse, saw him
and yelled out to him, "Sal si puedes! (Get out if you
can!)" which was not very helpful. The creek has been
so named ever since. That is what the flesh is like. We
struggle to correct these tendencies ourselves, but we
cannot do it. Only God has the wisdom to do it. That is

why Jeremiah's word in the tenth chapter comes to mind again. He said, "I know, O Lord, that the way of man is not in himself, that it is not in man who walks to direct his steps." And we are driven again to the wisdom of the Proverbs:

> Trust in the Lord with all your heart,
>   and lean not unto your own understanding.
> In all your ways acknowledge him,
>   and he shall direct your paths (Prov. 3:5–6, KJV).

Nothing else will do it. Your own heart will deceive you. If you follow your own desires, your own likings, you will end up trapped. Only the wisdom of the Word, only an honest acknowledgment of what is going on in your life will suffice. Bring it to God and tell him the whole thing, and trust him to have put your flesh to death on his cross. And rely upon his resurrection from there on, upon his power and his grace to lead you through. It is his knowledge of this tendency of the flesh which has led our Lord to include in the Lord's Prayer the little phrase which I pray every day, and I hope you do too: "Lead us not into temptation."

14

Now Hear This!

The Book of Jeremiah closes with a series of messages addressed to the nations around Israel. When as a teenager he was called to be a prophet, God had said to him, "See, I have set you this day over nations and over kingdoms, to pluck up and to break down." Now we see Jeremiah sending messages to the various nations around Israel regarding their destinies. There are three such collections of messages to the nations in the Scriptures. Isaiah has one series—many of them to the same nations addressed by Jeremiah—and the other is found in Ezekiel. All three taken together comprise a tremendous amount of Scripture, about 603 verses altogether—longer than many of the books of the New Testament. Yet I wonder how many Christians could pass an exam on what God has said to the nations through these great prophets.

Jeremiah begins with Egypt, where he himself was living at the time he compiled this series, and ends far to the east in the land of Babylon, across the Euphrates River. As we look at this section, we will see once again that truth in the Scriptures comes to us at several levels of understanding and application. First there is the historical, national, and political level of understanding this passage. These prophecies have to do with actual nations. God has said various things about them. Four of them he says will endure throughout time, and at the end of their history God will restore their fortunes and bless them. Those four nations are still existing today, and have in fact awakened from the dust of centuries and come to life again in these last few decades. Of two other nations nothing is said of ultimate blessing, although they still remain today. And three of these nations God specifically says shall disappear from the face of the earth. They have long since been lost to history.

There is another level at which this truth can be understood. On the historical level these nations come and go as God wills. But this address to the nations can also be understood as symbolizing, or typifying, forces at work within *us*. We will see this as we go through the account. These nine nations fall into three groups, each with extremely significant application to each of us. That is how we will approach them. We will begin with chapter 46, where we have Jeremiah's word to Egypt, comprising two messages he gave on two different occasions.

> The word of the Lord which came to Jeremiah the prophet concerning the nations. About Egypt. Concerning the army of Pharaoh Neco, king of Egypt, which was by the river Euphrates at Carchemish and which Nebuchadrezzar king of Babylon defeated in the fourth year of Jehoiakim the son of Josiah, king of Judah . . . (Jer. 46:1–2).

This takes us back to the year 605 B.C., when Nebuchadnezzar first came up against Judah. He was met by the armies of Egypt at the city of Carchemish on the Euphrates River, and there one of the great strategic battles of all history was fought. Until then, Egypt had been the most powerful nation of the day, but Babylon broke the power of Egypt at that place. Here Jeremiah is describing that battle in advance—how long in advance we do not know. He describes in very vivid terms the advance of the Babylonian army, the clash of these conflicting forces, the terrible battle that ensued, and the final defeat of Egypt.

Alluring Bondage

In the midst of this description, a characterization is made of Egypt. In the Scriptures Egypt is a picture of the world and its influence upon us. Egypt was a place of tyranny and bondage for the people of Israel. They were under the yoke of a wicked and severe king who enslaved them and treated them cruelly. Yet strangely enough, after they escaped, it was the place they always fondly remembered and wanted to return to. They remembered the food, the comfort, and the ease of life in Egypt. So this has always stood as a picture of the lure of the world to the believer—to think as it thinks, to react as it reacts, to seek one's own satisfaction and pleasure and enjoyment instead of living for the glory of God.

Now, when I refer to "the world" I am not talking about people, nor about doing any specific so-called "worldly" thing. That is not what worldliness is. Worldliness is an attitude of life that causes you to think of living only for your own pleasures and enjoyment. That is what Egypt symbolizes in Scripture. The character of Egypt is described for us in verses 7 and 8:

> "Who is this, rising like the Nile,
>   like rivers whose waters surge?

> Egypt rises like the Nile,
> like rivers whose waters surge."

Every spring the Nile River rises and overflows its banks, and this restores Egypt. The prophet uses this as a picture of the way the world comes at us—in surges and waves. We think we have it licked, but pretty soon it will come at us again. Repeatedly, again and again throughout our lifetime as believers on our spiritual pilgrimage, the world rises to afflict us and to lure us, and seeks to betray us and get us back into bondage again.

But there is another message here about Egypt, verses 13 to 24, delivered by Jeremiah after he had gone into exile in Egypt. Here he describes the forthcoming invasion of Egypt by Nebuchadnezzar, which took place after Jeremiah's death. In accordance with this prophecy, Nebuchadnezzar came down into Egypt and took over the land. In the midst of this prophecy is another characterization of Egypt, verse 17:

> "Call the name of Pharaoh, king of Egypt,
> 'Noisy one who lets the hour go by.' "

Isn't that a strange name to give somebody? In other words, "the noisy one who likes to kill time." That is the characterization of Egypt—and the world. It is one of the ways we can recognize the world: it loves noise, because it does not want to stop and think. And it loves to kill time, is always seeking ways to pass the time. Just recently I clipped an editorial from *Christianity Today:*

> Picture, if you will, some solar ray suddenly causing all radios, cassette players, stereo sets and televisions to stop working. Trembling hands impatiently twirl dials, adjust knobs, flip switches. Eyes are dilated with fear. Breathing comes in

spasms. Marx was wrong. Religion isn't the opiate of modern man; incessant sound is. We'll listen to anything to avoid silence—long pointless talk shows, boring conversations, round-the-clock news, and even rock and country music. We like sound because it blocks out the despairing cry of our own souls, as well as the still, small voice of God. But we need occasionally to take God's hand and journey into the fearful land of silence. It can be both painful and healing—with the presence of the One who is able to still the despairing cry, and give us a new song of thanks.

Yes, that is the world. It comes at us constantly, trying to get us to think only in terms of immediate pleasure and indulgence, and to forget that it leads to slavery and bondage. So God punishes Egypt—that is the message here.

Yet, on a national level, a strange word is said in verse 26:

> "I will deliver them [Egypt] into the hands of those who seek their life, into the hand of Nebuchadrezzar king of Babylon and his officers. Afterward Egypt shall be inhabited as in the days of old, says the Lord."

This undoubtedly is a reference to our own times when, after having lost its national standing and slept for centuries, Egypt has awakened, and is now a sovereign nation again. So God promises to spare Egypt. And in a similar message in Isaiah 19, God even says that eventually Egypt is going to be healed, and that he will bless them and call them his people.

In chapter 47 we have a message to a nation very closely associated with Egypt—Philistia. Do you remem-

ber your Bible stories about how the Philistines were
always coming up against Israel? Goliath, whom David
slew, was one of the Philistine warriors. These people
lived along the southern coastline of the land of Palestine.
In fact the name, "Palestine," comes from the word
Philistine. They were always the enemies of Israel. Many
scholars feel that originally they came from Egypt and
occupied Phoenicia, or Lebanon, as we know it today.
The Philistines were in the land, but they were the
enemies of God. Thus they are a symbol, or type, of the
worldling who claims a place in the land of promise, that
is, a nominal Christian who is nevertheless the enemy of
true faith. They are also a picture of those same attitudes
in our own lives and hearts—the tendency to want to enjoy the blessing of God in a given area of our life, but
without any heart commitment to him regarding that
area. Philistia is promised destruction:

The word of the Lord that came to Jeremiah the prophet
concerning the Philistines, before Pharaoh smote Gaza,

"Thus says the Lord:
Behold, waters are rising out of the north,
    and shall become an overflowing torrent;
they shall overflow the land and all that fills it,
    the city and those who dwell in it.
Men shall cry out,
    and every inhabitant of the land shall wail.
At the noise of the stamping of the hoofs of his stallions,
    at the rushing of his chariots,
    at the rumbling of their wheels,
the fathers look not back to their children,
    so feeble are their hands,
because of the day that is coming to destroy
    all the Philistines,

to cut off from Tyre and Sidon
  every helper that remains."

Here is the advance of the Babylonian army, which meant
the end of the nation of the Philistines.

"For the Lord is destroying the Philistines,
  the remnant of the coastland of Caphtor" (Jer. 47:1–4).

And so this nation perished, never to emerge again among
the nations of the world as a sovereign people.

Beginning in chapter 48 we have another group of
nations coming before us. Egypt and Philistia represent
the world in its enmity against us as believers. Now we
have five nations—Moab, Ammon, Edom, Damascus, and
Kedor, or Arabia—that represent something else. The
link between them is that all five are somehow related to
Israel. Thus they picture for us what the Bible calls "the
flesh"—that part of our nature which is inherent in us,
to which we are related, from which we cannot escape.
Yet it is the enemy of faith, the enemy of our lives, an
inner enemy.

Sons of Lot

Moab and Ammon occupy all of chapter 48 and the
first six verses of chapter 49, where we are given a
description of the character and of the downfall of these
nations. Moab and Ammon were the sons of Lot by his
own daughters. In that terrible story of the destruction of
Sodom and Gomorrah, when Lot and his daughters fled
from the city, we are told that later they got him drunk
so that he would lie with them and they could conceive
by him. Moab and Ammon settled in what is the present
land of Jordan—Moab to the east of the Dead Sea, and

Ammon north of Moab. Chapter 48 opens with a very
vivid description of the cities of Moab as they are assaulted one by one by the advance of the armies of Babylon. Then verse 11 says,

"Moab has been at ease from his youth
    and has settled on his lees;
[That is, he is resting on his rear end, his buttocks—"lees"
    is much more polite!]
he has not been emptied from vessel to vessel,
    nor has he gone into exile;
so his taste remains in him,
    and his scent is not changed."

Moab happened to be off the beaten track. Therefore the
conquerors who passed through this area century after
century left Moab alone. It had never been attacked, had
never been "emptied from vessel to vessel," from conqueror to conqueror, as the prophet says here. It had never
had its mouth go dry with fear. That is what "his taste
remains in him" means. And "his scent is not changed"
means he had never sweat with terror, thus changing his
odor. Moab had never known attack like this, so it was
complacent, confident, proud, and self-satisfied. Moab
therefore is a picture of the flesh in its confidence, its
cocksureness. "Everything is well, nothing is going to go
wrong." This pictures for us that attitude within us. But
God says,

> "Therefore, behold, the days are coming, says
> the Lord, when I shall send to him tilters who will
> tilt him, and empty his vessels, and break his jars
> in pieces. Then Moab shall be ashamed of
> Chemosh [their god], as the house of Israel
> was ashamed of Bethel, their confidence" (vss.
> 12–13).

Bethel was the place where Israel had worshiped two golden calves. God says he is going to disturb the confidence of Moab, is going to tilt him by the power of another nation. The reason is given in verses 29 and 30:

"We have heard of the pride of Moab—
   he is very proud—
of his loftiness, his pride, and his arrogance,
   and the haughtiness of his heart.
I know his insolence, says the Lord;
   his boasts are false,
   his deeds are false."

Whenever you feel that way about yourself, it is Moab attacking you, just as the Moabites constantly attacked Israel. You are contending with this continual enemy of God—the arrogance and insolence of the flesh. But eventual judgment is to fall upon them, nevertheless, as a nation, and finally there is this promise, verse 47: "Yet I will restore the fortunes of Moab in the latter days, says the Lord." Thus we have seen Jordan emerge as a nation in our own time.

Connected with Moab is Ammon, to the north. The present capital of Jordan is Amman. Typologically, Ammon stands for the same as Moab, but with one addition: it is more aggressive, more warlike than Moab. It represents that insolence and arrogance which preys upon the spirit within us. Yet the promise to this nation, along with Moab, is this: "But afterward I will restore the fortunes of the Ammonites, says the Lord" (Jer. 49:6). Therefore as a people and a nation they still exist in the world.

The Calamity of Esau

In verses 7 through 22 we have the prophecy against Edom, which occupied the land south of the Dead Sea.

For many centuries its capital was Petra, that beautiful city carved out of red rock. Edom was a descendant of Esau, the twin brother of Jacob. In Scripture, Esau is always a picture of the man of the flesh, especially as the flesh opposes and is contrary to the Spirit. "Jacob have I loved," God said, "Esau have I hated." And in the Book of Galatians, Paul contrasts these two: "For the desires of the flesh are against the Spirit, and the desires of the Spirit are against the flesh; for these are opposed to each other . . ." In chapter 49, God promises to eliminate this nation completely. Look at verses 8 through 10:

> "Flee, turn back, dwell in the depths,
> 　O inhabitants of Dedan!
> For I will bring the calamity of Esau upon him,
> 　the time when I punish him,
> If grape-gatherers came to you,
> 　would they not leave gleanings?
> If thieves came by night,
> 　would they not destroy only enough for themselves?
> But I have stripped Esau bare,
> 　I have uncovered his hiding places,
> 　and he is not able to conceal himself.
> His children are destroyed, and his brothers,
> 　and his neighbors; and he is no more."

True to this word, the nation of Edom passed from the stage of history long before the time of our Lord. It lost its national standing and disappeared in the dust of the centuries, never to emerge again.

The last two nations in this group are given from verse 23 on: first Damascus, and then Kedar, which is another name for Arabia—the Bedouin tribes who inhabited the desert areas of what is now called Saudi Arabia. Nothing is said of ultimate promise to these nations, although they are permitted to continue. But judgment is visited upon them—Damascus first, and then the Arabian nations, who were descended from Ishmael, the half-brother of Isaac, son of Abraham. Thus they too are related to Israel. In vivid language the prophet describes the destruction as the armies of Babylon come up to Damascus, verses 25 and 26:

"How the famous city is forsaken,
    the joyful city!
Therefore her young men shall fall in her squares,
    and all her soldiers shall be destroyed in that day,
                        says the Lord of hosts."

The Arabian tribes also are afflicted, verse 29:

"Their tents and their flocks shall be taken,
    their curtains and all their goods;
their camels shall be borne away from them,
    and men shall cry to them, 'Terror on every side!' "

Thus these nations are judged by God. Typologically, they represent the restlessness of our natures, and the power to upset and disarrange us which that restlessness creates within us. Wherever these nations appear in Scripture, that is what they stand for. One of the clues to understanding the Word of God is to see yourself whenever you read about these nations. We can understand how we operate, as we see it in the national lives of these people. Thus the marks of the flesh are judged.

The last two nations are associated—Elam and Babylon. The word about Elam is given to us in the closing words of chapter 49, beginning at verse 34. At this time it was one of the provinces of Babylon, and yet it is singled out here by Jeremiah as meriting a very signifi-

cant word from God. The reason is given in verses 34
and 35:

> The word of the Lord that came to Jeremiah
> the prophet concerning Elam, in the beginning of
> the reign of Zedekiah king of Judah.
> Thus says the Lord of hosts: "Behold, I will
> break the bow of Elam, the mainstay of their
> might . . ."

Elam is characterized by a bow, which is called the
"mainstay" of Elam. A bow, of course, is a symbol of
the ability to strike and injure at a distance. Typologically, it stands for what Paul calls "the fiery darts of the
wicked one" which are hurled at us, the evil thoughts and
imaginations which come unbidden into our hearts and
minds—sometimes when we least expect them. You kneel
to pray, and you are appalled at the evil thought which
suddenly possesses your mind. What is that? One of the
fiery darts of the wicked one. Just when you are rejoicing
in the blessing of God, some stupid, silly doubt suddenly
possesses your heart, and you wonder whether you are
really a Christian or not. What is that? Another of the
fiery darts of the wicked one, the bow and arrows of Elam
which are the mainstay of this enemy of God, and God
pronounces judgment upon them. Nevertheless, on the
national level, note verse 39: "But in the latter days I will
restore the fortunes of Elam, says the Lord." Elam today
is the land of Iran, or Persia, and has emerged again as a
sovereign nation, in accordance with this word.

Chapters 50 and 51, two of the longest in the book, are
devoted to the destruction and overthrow of Babylon. I
hardly need comment on what Babylon stands for. Everywhere in Scripture it is a symbol of the great enemy of

God, called in Revelation "that old serpent the devil," especially as the devil uses false religious authority to claim earthly standing, prestige, and power. That is Babylonianism.

Fountainhead of Idolatry

Do you remember where Babylon began? In the tower of Babel, after the Flood. And why did men erect the tower of Babel? The Genesis account says, ". . . in order that they might make a name for themselves." Babylonianism is the attempt to gain some prestige or status in the eyes of the world by the use of religious authority. You can see that it has permeated every religious group, every denomination, every church. Every religion in the world seeks that. We struggle with Babylonianism right here at Peninsula Bible Church. Any time we long to be known around the world, to exercise particular prestige in our community, that is Babylonianism at work. It has seized whole systems of religion so that these systems seek to gain great authority, to be known as princes and kings and powers in the world today. It all began with the tower of Babel.

At Babel, men erected a tower in order to ascend into the heavens and become like God. And under Nimrod the city became the mother of harlots and the abominations of the earth. That is, it became the fountainhead of idolatry and began to export these ideas all throughout the world. If you want to study this more fully, I suggest you read Alexander Hislop's book, *The Two Babylons*, tracing how these foul ideas began in Babylon and spread throughout the whole earth.

The prophet predicts the historical overthrow of the

city by the Medes and the Persians, beginning at verse 2 of chapter 50:

"Decline among the nations and proclaim,
  set up a banner and proclaim,
  conceal it not, and say:
'Babylon is taken,
  Bel [Baal] is put to shame,
Merodach [Marduk, another name for Baal] is dismayed.
Her images are put to shame,
  her idols are dismayed.'
  "For out of the north a nation has come up against her, which shall make her land a desolation, and none shall dwell in it; both man and beast shall flee away" (Jer. 50:2–3).

Just as Babylon itself was the great destructive power against Judah, so Babylon's turn must come. Out of the north, the Medes and the Persians will come against Babylon and overthrow this great kingdom. Despite its tremendous walls, its vast palaces, its ornate hanging gardens, its huge size, and its great armies—the greatest power of the world of that day—at the very height of its power God declares that it shall be totally lost to sight. Even its site would be lost to men. It would be "a desolation, and none shall dwell in it."

In verses 4 and 5 we read of the return of the Jews to the land of Judah:

"In those days and in that time, says the Lord, the people of Israel and the people of Judah shall come together, weeping as they come; and they shall seek the Lord their God. They shall ask the way to Zion, with faces turned toward it, saying,

'Come, let us join ourselves to the Lord in an ever-lasting covenant which will never be forgotten.' "

Thus they came back from exile into the land. But Babylon's overthrow is going to be total. Look at verses 12 and 13:

". . . your mother [i.e., the mother of all harlotry] shall be
    utterly shamed,
  and she who bore you shall be disgraced.
Lo, she shall be the last of the nations,
  a wilderness dry and desert.
Because of the wrath of the Lord she shall not be inhabited,
  but shall be an utter desolation;
every one who passes by Babylon shall be appalled,
  and hiss [or whistle] because of all her wounds."

Verses 39 and 40:

"Therefore wild beasts shall dwell with hyenas
in Babylon, and ostriches shall dwell in her; she
shall be peopled no more for ever, nor inhabited for
all generations. As when God overthrew Sodom
and Gomorrah and their neighbor cities, says the
Lord, so no man shall dwell there, and no son of
man shall sojourn in her."

The Book of Daniel tells us that king Belshazzar made a great feast, inviting all the lords of Babylon to the palace. As they were reveling in drunken debauchery, a hand appeared and wrote on the wall. Do you remember that dramatic incident? The king trembled, and Daniel was called in to interpret the writing. And Daniel told him that that night the kingdom would be taken from him. And that night Darius the Mede led his armies into Babylon, and the kingdom was overthrown. There is a reference to that in verse 43 here:

> "The king of Babylon heard the report of them,
>   and his hands fell helpless;
> anguish seized him,
>   pain as of a woman in travail."

So the great city was overthrown, and was so completely demolished that the site was abandoned and never rebuilt. The dust of the ages covered it over, and for centuries the actual site of this great city was lost, so that men did not even know where it was. It was only at the beginning of the present century that its site was unearthed, and once again the walls and vestigial remains of the city are coming into the light of day. But as God said, it had become a desert and a desolate place. The silent mounds beside the Euphrates River bore eloquent testimony to the truth of the Scriptures. Verses 31 and 32:

> "Behold, I am against you, O proud one,
>   says the Lord God of hosts;
> for your day has come,
>   the time when I will punish you.
> The proud one shall stumble and fall,
>   with none to raise him up,
> and I will kindle a fire in his cities,
>   and it will devour all that is round about him."

There are many who say that Babylon must be built again—you can read this in some books which are in circulation today—because of the prophecies in the Book of Revelation that refer to Babylon. But you need to note that the reference there is to "Mystery Babylon the great." This is not the actual, literal city, but that for which Babylon stands—the idolatrous practices and the blas-

phemous assumption of power by religious authority.
This is what is going to be destroyed, as the Book of
Revelation says. To picture that destruction, John bor-
rows words from Jeremiah's description of the literal
destruction of the city of Babylon, chapter 51, verse 6:

> "Flee from the midst of Babylon,
>   let every man save his life!
> Be not cut off in her punishment,
>   for this is the time of the Lord's vengeance,
>   the requital he is rendering her.
> Babylon was a golden cup in the Lord's hand,
>   making all the earth drunken;
> the nations drank of her wine,
>   therefore the nations went mad.
> Suddenly Babylon has fallen and been broken;
>   wail for her!" (Jer. 51:6–8).

And so the great city perished. But God has this final
word to say, beginning at verse 59:

> The word which Jeremiah the prophet com-
> manded Seraiah the son of Neriah, son of Mah-
> seiah, when he went with Zedekiah king of
> Judah to Babylon, in the fourth year of his reign.
> Seraiah was the quartermaster. [That is, Seraiah
> went down to Babylon as an ambassador from
> Judah.] Jeremiah wrote in a book all the evil that
> should come upon Babylon, all these words that
> are written concerning Babylon. And Jeremiah
> said to Seraiah: "When you come to Babylon, see
> that you read all these words [you see, Babylon has
> heard this], and say, 'O Lord, thou hast said con-
> cerning this place that thou wilt cut it off, so that
> nothing shall dwell in it. Neither man nor beast,
> and it shall be desolate for ever.' When you finish
> reading this book, bind a stone to it, and cast it

into the midst of the Euphrates, and say, 'Thus shall Babylon sink, to rise no more, because of the evil that I am bringing upon her' " (Jer. 51:59–64).

This is the end of the words of Jeremiah. According to. Jewish tradition, he died in Egypt, martyred at the hands of his own countrymen. The final chapter is a historical summary appended by another hand, recounting the fall of Jerusalem and the ultimate restoration of king Jehoiachin in the city of Babylon.

What is the message of this book to us? We have gone through it, and have watched this prophet in his struggles with the ways and the workings of God, and have seen our own struggles reflected there. What is the great message which abides in this book? Surely it is contained in these messages to the nations. Here are groups of nations which symbolize the enemy arrayed against us: the devil, and the two channels through which he attacks us —the world and the flesh. And God's Word says that God is adequate for all of them. Faith in a living God can overcome the world, can beat back the deceitfulness of the flesh, and can overcome the roaring, lionlike qualities of the devil in our life, so that we can stand—God's man, God's woman—free in the midst of the bondage of this age.

Babylon shall sink and never rise again. In the closing chapter of Romans, Paul promises that God shall come and crush Satan under our feet. May that be our experience now in these days. These are forces with great power, bringing to pass all the terrible things recorded in our daily newspapers. But by faith we can walk in the midst of them. That is God's message in the Book of Jeremiah.